POST-WAR ON THE LINERS

POST-WAR ON THE LINERS

WILLIAM H. MILLER

FONTHILL

For Tim Noble—friend, ship buff, officer of merchant ships

Fonthill Media Language Policy

Fonthill Media publishes in the international English language market. One language edition is published worldwide. As there are minor differences in spelling and presentation, especially with regard to American English and British English, a policy is necessary to define which form of English to use. The Fonthill Policy is to use the form of English native to the author. William H. Miller was born and educated in the USA and now lives in Secaucus, New Jersey, therefore American English has been adopted in this publication.

Fonthill Media Limited
Fonthill Media LLC
www.fonthillmedia.com
office@fonthillmedia.com

First published in the United Kingdom
and the United States of America 2015

British Library Cataloguing in Publication Data:
A catalogue record for this book is available from the British Library

Typeset in 11pt on 13pt Minion Pro
Printed and bound in England

CONTENTS

ACKNOWLEDGMENTS

Like the operation of a passenger ship, many hands have assisted in the production of this book. I a merely the chief purser, who organizes the people, the contents, the selection of material, the quotes and comments, as well as the illustrations.

First of all, I'd like to extend my great appreciation to Fonthill Media for taking on this project, and to Jay Slater and Jasper Hadman; to the superbly talented Stephen Card for his wonderful covers; to Michael Hadgis for his technical expertise and advice; to Tim Noble for his great help; Harry Benson for his Foreword; and, for great and continued photographic assistance, Richard Faber, Anthony La Forgia, Captain James McNamara, and Albert Wilhelmi.

Other much valued contributors include James Andrews, Ernest Arroyo, Captain Adriano Borreani, Philippe Brebant, James Buchannan, Mary Burns, Peter Buttfield, Captain Lorenzo Calvillo, the late Douglas Campbell, Luis Miguel Correia, the late Frank Cronican, the late Alex Duncan, Maurizio Eliseo, Ugo Frangini, Howard Franklin, Geoff Gardner, the late John Gillespie, the late Lewis and Ruth Gordon, Brian Gregory, Joann Hastings, Andy Hernandez, Keith Hickey, Pine Hodges, the late F. Leonard Jackson, Lindsay Johnstone, John Jones, the late Andrew Kilk, Peter Knego, Mike McDougle, John Morgan, George Munn, Mark Nemergut, Hisashi Noma, Robert Pabst, Alan Partkhurst, Michael Parks, Paolo Piccione, George Pilgrim, the late Ron Peach, Roger Sherlock, John Spooner, Steffen Weirauch, John Williams, and the late Len Wilton.

Companies and other organizations that have assisted include British India Line, Companhia Colonial, Cunard Line, Halifax Maritime Museum, Holland America Line, Moran Towing & Transportation Company, P&O, Shaw Savill Line, Steamship Historical Society of America, United States Lines, World Ocean & Cruise Liner Society, and World Ship Society.

FOREWORD

Having worked as a steward for P&O until the late 1960s, I traveled the world aboard some of their great liners—the *Himalaya, Iberia, Oronsay, Orsova, Cathay*, and *Canberra*. We visited some of the biggest and busiest ports. I remember the docks at London and Southampton well, both of which seemed crammed with passenger ships. When we would sail, say, from Southampton, there might be liners belonging to Cunard, Union-Castle, Royal Mail, Shaw Savill, and any number of foreign-flag lines. At Sydney, we would see ships flying the flags of those foreign lines as well—with names like Lloyd Triestino, Sitmar, and Chandris. Sometimes we would pass other liners in the Suez or Panama Canals or meet at anchorages at places like Aden, Trinidad, and Port Suez. Those liners, all now gone, offered a global network of services. You could sail almost anywhere on a passenger ship. Of course, we had all types of passengers—from the titled rich in top-deck first class to the poorest of migrants down on the lowest deck in tourist class. We would have passengers traveling with those bygone steamer trunks and changing clothes three and four times a day, while others had little more than one suitcase and one set of clothes.

I miss those days—it was another era, a golden age in many ways. I have attended Bill Miller's fascinating and fact-filled lectures mostly aboard the current Cunard liners—the *Queen Mary 2, Queen Victoria*, and *Queen Elizabeth*. His talks sparked many memories, making me feel quite nostalgic. Therefore, it is with pleasure and gratitude that I write this Foreword introducing the last great age of the passenger liner, those post-war years from the late 1940s through to the 1970s.

Harry Benson
London, England
Fall 2014

Gala departure: Farewell to the *President Cleveland* at San Francisco, 1955. (*Richard Faber Collection*)

INTRODUCTION

By the late summer of 1945, the victorious powerhouse of America was calming down. The War was over and America was the uncontested leader of the Allied victors. After spending billions of dollars on the war effort, America still had billions. Across the seas, much of Europe was in ruins. Germany had been, almost deservedly, flattened, while Britain and France were all but bankrupt. The likes of Italy, Holland, and Poland were deeply wounded. They were nations of great hungry masses, flattened cities, and devastated industries. On the other side of globe, Japan was gasping its last breaths. Indeed, there was great flux and change was anticipated throughout the world. The Dutch East Indies would very shortly cast off the yoke of Dutch colonial rule and re-invent itself as Indonesia. India would soon follow, tossing away its British parentage.

The War had also created huge social turmoil. The poor and hungry of Europe, for example, found little in their homelands and so looked elsewhere—to America in particular, but also to Canada, South America, South Africa, and Australia. Tens of thousands sought transport to make their migration, and almost all travelled by ship. From resuscitated pre-war liners to aged steamers, kept alive beyond their years, and spartanly converted cargo ships. Then there were the refugees, the displaced persons, the survivors of the notorious Nazi camps—people who had no homes or homeland. Great waves of people, many with little or no luggage, found their way to docksides in London, Rotterdam, Bremerhaven, Lisbon, and Genoa, and there boarded ships on their 'voyages of a lifetime'—voyages that might

well bring new lives with freedom, hope and, perhaps most of all, economic opportunity. Heading to New York, it was the Ellis Island process from the first decades of the twentieth century brought forward.

Decades later, I met a woman, by then gray haired and reflective, who left her native Holland in 1948. There was little food, no money and very few jobs, she told me, and in whispers there was talk of another great war, a conflict that might turn all of Europe into a Soviet-Communist satellite. Still hungry and with very little money, she managed a ticket for a nine-day voyage from war-damaged Rotterdam to Halifax, the port of entry for a 'new life' in Canada. The ship, dating from 1922, already seemed very old and quite basic, she told me. There were 2,000 migrants on board, with very few in actual cabins, but most people were accommodated in dormitories, some with as many as fifty or sixty bunks. Some of the spaces looked as if they had been mere carryovers from the ship's use during the War as an Allied troopship and when she sometimes carried three to four thousand men. There were many Dutch, but also Germans, Austrians, Danes, Czechs and even some Italians among the passengers. The woman spoke several languages and so was soon discovered by the ship's officer-in-charge as the ideal interpreter, not only in explaining the ways of the ship, no matter how simple, but in the preparation of paperwork for the passengers' entry into Canada. Food was very, very simple, she told me, but then much of Holland had been starving almost to death in the bitter winter and spring of

1945. Those passengers were hardly particular, she reported. Every passenger was also given one apple per day. Her role as a shipboard interpreter warranted a reward of sorts. She was given a second apple each day, and decades later it was still a proud memory. Life was very simple, she told me, and that second apple was, in ways, like a gold coin.

The post-war years also saw the great and, in many cases, grand resumption of passenger ship services. There were businessmen, government officials, the rebuilders and restorers. And, on the famed Atlantic run, there was the return of the celebrities—film stars, politicians, even royalty. Traveling in grand style awoke from its dormancy since the final days of that peaceful summer of 1939. The collections of vast trunks returned, personal servants in tow, with maybe a big American car stowed in the ship's hold.

The dirt and dust and rubble of the War seemed to have been cleared away by the end of the 1940s, even beginning in 1947. Ship owners almost everywhere, in London, Liverpool, Paris, Antwerp, Lisbon, Rome, and even Hamburg, began to make plans, if only in pencil, for a new age of sea-going prosperity. They felt confident there would be more and more passengers, and so new, possibly bigger and improved passenger ships would be needed. Alone, Britain's P&O and Orient Lines, long dominant in the UK-to-Australia trade, made plans for no less than seven liners, the smallest being 24,000 tons and the largest nearly 30,000. These were large liners at that time and most of them carrying as many as 1,500 passengers.

Then, of course, there were compensations, mostly from generous government ministries, for the staggering losses during the War years. Sometimes entire fleets had to be replaced. Between 1947 and 1953, the Union-Castle Line, Britain's dominant carrier in the African trades, planned for no less than six new liners. Emerging from its own rubble, the Italians looked to a quartet of large, quite luxurious liners—two for the run to South America and two, larger, faster and more luxurious, for the prestigious, highly competitive link to New York. Shipyards were, in some cases, overcrowded. Considering the massive rebuilding of cargo ship fleets, there were waitlists for new tonnage. In Britain, there were also waitlists for the likes of government-controlled steel allocations.

On the famed and well-documented North Atlantic run, over a third of the passenger ships from 1939 were gone, destroyed in the War. A few ships were missing for other reasons, such as not being returned from lingering government duties until as late as 1950–51. Others such as Cunard's pre-war *Alaunia* had been drastically altered, having been reconstructed as a military repair ship, a 'floating shipyard'. She never rejoined the company's commercial fleet. Many of the very famous super liners were gone as well. Defeated Germany was stripped completely while Italy was humbled and had only four large liners remaining. The much-reduced French had but two. Big, fast, and luxurious ocean liners were actually very few in number. There was the *Queen Mary* and *Queen Elizabeth*, both heroic veterans of the War when, painted in somber grays, they transported millions across the Atlantic for the eventual, very decisive invasion at Normandy in June 1944. Then there was the much-neglected *Europa*, all but unused during the War by the Nazi high command and taken as a trophy when Yankee soldiers marched into Bremerhaven in May 1945. Later, when she was found to be unacceptable to American safety standards, she was given to the French to become the much renewed, revitalized *Liberté*. Far off, the devastated Japanese had but one surviving passenger ship, the very meager, 11,000-ton *Hikawa Maru*.

By the 1950s, it was 'full steam ahead'. There were more and more passenger ships, including lots of brand new ones, a few innovative ones and, of course, a seemingly limitless flow of passengers. Many ships were booked months, even a year in advance. Prospects for the future looked not only good, but very good as far as the 1960s and beyond.

While air travel actually began creeping in further and further by the mid-1950s, it was the very first trans-Atlantic jet flights in October 1958 that began the dramatic and devastating decline of passenger ship services between Europe and North America. Within six months, by mid-1959, the airlines had two-thirds of all the business, from gold-plated first class travelers to those bargain basement travelers down in tourist class. Within five years, by 1963, the airlines had brutally snatched as much as 98 per cent of all Atlantic passengers. I recall the otherwise legendary *Queen Mary* once arriving in New York in 1964 with a paltry 175 passengers and 1,200-person crew. Other less-celebrated liners such as the *Carinthia*, another Cunarder, put into New York with 90 passengers (and 450 crew) and even the cheap, almost all-tourist class *Arosa Star* arrived with 25 against a full capacity of well over 800. Some companies faded away and others greatly contracted; some ships, such as Cunard's once very popular

Mauretania, had to cancel crossings to New York. There were simply not enough passengers.

Steamship line directors, operations staff, the new age of the 'sales and marketing department', and all-round visionaries looked to new ideas, new ventures, new services. With the last vestiges of Holland's colonial trade greatly withered, the likes of the Nederland Line and Royal Rotterdam Lloyd combined forces to create a 'new' tourist service: largely inexpensive three-month around-the-world voyages. From its otherwise staid, wood-paneled headquarters in London, the now combined P&O-Orient Lines saw the Pacific as the 'last frontier' of expansionist liner trade. Beginning in the late 1950s, increasing numbers of sailings were routed across the Pacific to and from the North American West Coast. Some ideas were, quite expectedly, unsuccessful, such as placing the aging *Mauretania* on the Mediterranean–New York route. It was long-unfamiliar territory for Cunard, and in fierce competition with the flashy, modern, brand new *Leonardo da Vinci*.

The ubiquitous 'silver tube', the increasingly larger and faster jet aircraft, waited ten years, until the late 1960s, before reaching, say, beyond Suez. Thereafter, it was 21 hours compared to 21 days on even a big, fast liner such as P&O's *Oriana*. It had all changed—and so abruptly, it seemed—as fast, affordable flights sprouted everywhere: Paris to Rio, London to Cape Town, Bombay, Sydney and Hong Kong, and Tokyo to San Francisco. Then, to complicate matters further, there was decolonization, the shift to so-called Third World ship owners and, with time passing, aging and therefore expensive passenger ships. Whole parades of ships, it seems, began their final voyages to the breakers' yards in Spain, Italy, Turkey, Japan, but mostly to Taiwan. On the high seas almost everywhere, the 'party' was all but over.

Then, in 1969, the highly questionable *Queen Elizabeth 2* appeared on the scene. 'What is Cunard thinking?' screamed one newspaper headline in the UK. But as countless passenger ships (as opposed to the increasingly popular and therefore far more profitable cruise ships) continue to steam off to the scrappers, and even as whole shipping lines themselves gasped their last breaths, the 1,700-bed *QE2*, as it was best known, sailed on and on—and for 39 years. Yes, there is a positive end to our story—that 'party' on the seas continued. These days, of course, it is in the hands of the even larger, 2,600-capacity *Queen Mary 2*.

As this latest Cunard flagship and superliner, the last 'true ocean liner' according to her owners, speeds across the North Atlantic between Southampton and New York, her foamy wake is a collection of ships, services and the countless passengers that sailed the seas particularly between 1945 and 1970.

Herein, I have listed and recounted only some of them, mostly included by choice; there were far too many passenger ships in the 1950s and '60s to be included in a single volume. Altogether, I hope the selected few will prove to be a most interesting collection of ships.

Bill Miller
Secaucus, New Jersey
Fall 2014

1

THE LATE 1940s:
ALL KINDS OF PASSENGERS, ALL KINDS OF SHIPS

The Duke and Duchess of Windsor were regular passengers on the North Atlantic, crossing twice each year in each direction. They used the Cunard *Queens* beginning in the late 1940s but then transferred their maritime affections to the speedy *United States*, beginning in the mid-1950s. They Windsors were reflective of the grandest way of travel—for their five-day passages, they never sailed with less than ninety-eight pieces of luggage including as many as thirty of those bulky trunks. Onboard the American flagship, they occupied an inter-connecting three-room suite and had three cabins across the corridor as well—singles for a butler, a maid, and the third used as a closet and pressing room for their vast wardrobes. They brought along personal furnishings, artistic objects, china, bed linen, and their five dogs. And there were others just like them. One European baroness reportedly crossed the Atlantic with six personal staff and 120 pieces of luggage.

At the opposite end were budget-minded travelers—teachers, students, and young tourists off on the classic holiday, and immigrants searching for a new life. They often traveled with very little luggage and shared cabins with as many as eight berths, or dormitories holding as many as forty or fifty other occupants.

In between, there were business people, comfort-seeking tourists, and families occupying several, sometimes inter-connecting cabins.

The migrant trades provided big, profitable business after the Second World War. There were Europeans seeking new and hopefully more prosperous lives in the likes of America, Australia, South Africa, and South America; Asians crossing the Pacific to North America; and more specific trades, such as East and West Indians heading to Britain.

New liners were built for these trades. Some were big ships with two or three classes of accommodation, while others were smaller, and some were practical blends of passenger and cargo—the popular 'combo' ships. Still others were very basic passenger ships, reconstructed from the hulls of freighters, troopships, and even small aircraft carriers.

Ships such as Cunard's *Queens* were lavishly and luxuriously restored. Another Cunarder, the *Caronia,* commissioned in 1948, had the amenity of having a private bathroom in every cabin despite class designation. The American liners *Independence* and *Constitution* of 1951 had the distinction of being the first fully air-conditioned liners. Cunard's *Georgic* had been bombed and heavily destroyed, but was repaired only to a troopship-like status. Despite her very basic condition and austere style, she was pressed into summer season trans-Atlantic service carrying almost 2,000 one-class passengers per crossing. Similarly, the Dutch *Groote Beer* and her two sisters, *Waterman* and *Zuiderkruis*, all converted freighters, carried migrants as well as students in accommodation that included 55-berth dormitories and large public bathroom facilities.

Altogether, business boomed. On a morning in 1957, for example, almost 10,000 passengers arrived in New York harbor. All of them arrived by passenger ships.

CUNARD LINE
CUNARD WHITE STAR
TRANSATLANTIC
and CRUISE
SAILINGS AND RATES
•
GENERAL INFORMATION

NUMBER 6
DECEMBER 17, 1951

R. M. S. CARONIA

BOOK THROUGH YOUR LOCAL TRAVEL AGENT
No one can serve you better

THE CUNARD STEAM-SHIP COMPANY LIMITED

Above: The first liner to return to trans-Atlantic service was Norway's *Stavangerfjord* in the summer of 1945. (*Author's Collection*)

Left: Picking a sailing to Europe on Cunard, 1951. (*Author's Collection*)

Below: The Duke and Duchess of Windsor in the sitting room of their Main Deck suite aboard the liner *United States*, May 1962. (*Mark Nemergut Collection*)

Above: Austere student and migrant ships such as the Dutch-flag *Groote Beer* were alternatives to the more luxurious liners. (*Holland America Line*)

Right: Bon Voyage! Seeing passengers off to Europe from the Manhattan piers was a tradition. (*Richard Faber Collection*)

s.s. GROOTE BEER
s.s. WATERMAN
s.s. ZUIDERKRUIS

NETHERLANDS GOVERNMENT VESSELS
Directorate-General of Shipping
(Ministerie van Verkeer en Waterstaat)

Holland-America Line, Agents

Above: Cunard's 13,500-ton, combination passenger-cargo liner *Media* was said to be the first new Atlantic liner following the War. She was commissioned in the summer of 1947. (*F. Leonard Jackson Collection*)

Left: It was $140 for nine days from New York to Rotterdam aboard these Dutch ships in the late 1950s. (*Author's Collection*)

Left: Holland America's *Ryndam* and *Maasdam* were sensations with their comfortable $20-a-day passages to and from Europe in the early 1950s. (*Author's Collection*)

Right: Another economy ship was West Germany's *Seven Seas*. She carried twenty in a small first class, but almost 1,000 in low-fare, lower deck tourist class. (*Author's Collection*)

2

TRANS-ATLANTIC:
SUMMER IN EUROPE

Marian, long retired and living in Maryland, told me she made as many as two dozen Atlantic crossings in the 1950s and '60s—all of them on liners. Her father and then her husband were university professors, so they sailed to and from Europe, England mostly, for their studies, research, and exchange teaching. She recalled those journeys clearly:

The SS *United States* was a very fast ship, only five days from New York to Southampton, but shook and rattled for four-and-a-half of those five days. I remember seeing the Duke of Windsor walking on the Promenade Deck (and wearing one of his very stylized suits and striped socks) and also Salvador Dali and his wife. On French liners, the *Ile de France, Liberté* and the *France*, the food was too wonderful. And we ate things we'd never heard of or even seen before. It was pure gourmet and just about impossible to eat less. There was also a mood, a more festive, happy tone, on the French ships that the other liners did not seem to have. In ways, it was like being in Paris. It was all fun, gay and stylish.

Otherwise, the big Cunarders seemed solid, were well run, but always rather staid and sometimes a little bit stuffy. I remember a very grand, old British lady in first class who suddenly stopped speaking to another woman when she discovered she was actually traveling down in tourist class. On Holland-America, the *Nieuw Amsterdam* and the *Maasdam* were immaculate. I seem to remember the Dutch crewmembers scrubbing the decks at five in the morning. And on the *Bremen*, there was still that heel-clicking, Germanic style. It was like some old film. I recall a German man strolling on deck with his leather trench coat draped over his shoulders and smoking cigarettes in a long, tortoise shell holder. And the very best looking stewards and waiters, it seemed, were on the *Bremen*. They could have all been movie stars, or so it appeared. Everything was absolutely precise on the *Bremen*, right down to the very orderly stacking of the towels in closets and lockers. That young actress Elke Sommer was aboard.

Not used very much during the Second World War, Norwegian America Line's 14,000-ton *Stavangerfjord* was cleaned, given a fresh coat of paint and readied for commercial service. When she set off from Oslo for New York in August 1945, she became the first liner to return to service after the War. Others gradually followed such as Holland America's 134-passenger *Westerdam* in the spring of 1946. The first new passenger ship to be launched after the War years (and when almost 50 per cent of the Atlantic liner fleet had been destroyed) was, in fact, a Swede, the 12,000-ton *Stockholm*. Although designed for Swedish American Line's mainline service between Gothenburg, Copenhagen, and New York, she was actually a combination passenger-cargo ship with only 400 passenger berths in all. The first brand new passenger ship to actually enter post-war Atlantic service was another combination type, Cunard's 250-passenger *Media*, which had its debut in August 1947. That 530-foot-long ship had space for 250 passengers, all of them in first class. Combination passenger-cargo liners were very popular following the Second World War. They were seen as an ideal economic balance—carrying one or two hundred passengers as well as a substantial amount of cargo.

Cunard Line

Just after the Second World War ended and throughout the 1950s, the Cunard *Queens*—the illustrious *Queen Mary* and *Queen Elizabeth*—were the most prominent, popular, and profitable big liners on the reviving trans-Atlantic service. Together, beginning in the summer of 1947, the fully restored and renovated super liners were unmatched on the so-called Atlantic Ferry. Usually booked to absolute capacity, they offered lavishly luxurious accommodation in first class, very comfortable but less expensive quarters in cabin class (akin to today's airline business class), and least expensive of all but still with adequate space, a lower-deck tourist class.

Off to sea! John Jones was a mere boy of fifteen when he walked into the huge and very grand Cunard offices in his native Liverpool.

A man that seemed to be 10 feet tall took me to a room, placed me against a wall and measured my height. Happily, I was just tall enough. I was soon off to training school and then assigned to the *Scythia*, then thirty years old and sailing on the Liverpool to Quebec City run. I earned 7 pounds a month or 5p an hour. I was given a crimson uniform and pillbox hat and off I went. After that, I had to buy my own uniforms from a London tailor on Saville Row. We were said to be the youngest seamen in the British merchant navy and, as a group, we slept ten to twelve to a room. We ran errands onboard, delivered telegrams and other messages, helped in the purser's office and sometimes sat and chatted with passengers, especially ladies in first class, who were traveling alone. One grand lady once had four bellboys sitting at her feet!

John was soon posted to another veteran Cunarder, the *Franconia*. 'She went aground in the St Lawrence, near Quebec City [July 1950], and then needed weeks of repairs. Many of the crew took jobs in the Chateau Frontenac Hotel to stay busy, but mostly to earn extra money.'

When James Andrews emigrated from war-ravaged England, where rations were still imposed, to a 'new life' in America in 1951, he landed at New York's Pier 90 aboard what was then the biggest ocean liner ever built, the 83,673-ton *Queen Elizabeth*. Capped by two large, orange-red and black funnels, she was 1,031 feet in length and could carry 2,233 passengers divided in those three classes. The *Queen Elizabeth* landed, as James recalled, 2,219 passengers, which was very close to absolute capacity. The *Queens* were often booked a year in advance; the airlines had yet to overtake the steamship companies and so the likes of the Cunard Steam-Ship Company Limited, as it was formally named, were highly profitable. In addition, the *Queens* alone were said to earn millions for the post-war British economy. With close to a dozen passenger ships of their own and therefore garnering the biggest chunk of all North Atlantic traffic, they enthusiastically boasted that 'Getting there was half the fun'. Indeed, it was. Hearty English breakfasts, shuffleboard and the mileage pool, ritualized afternoon teas, a good book in one of those wooden deck chairs, and all while tucked-in by a cheerful attendant steward with a great Tartan blanket, which the British (and Cunard) called 'rugs'. For Americans, it was very often the beginning of a European visit—those fabled 'summers in Europe'—and then, on the return crossing, a rest after weeks and sometimes months of hotel rooms, tour guides, visits to museums, cathedrals and ancient ruins. Then, of course, also onboard were the glamorous Hollywood stars, the front-page politicians, the corporate chiefs, even royalty. They used the Cunarders—as the *Queens* were dubbed—for pure but very pampered transport. But like James Andrews's voyage in the *Queen Elizabeth*, it was still transport—delivering passengers from Point A to Point B.

James Buchannan recalls his memories of the Queens with fondness:

The two, big *Queens* were marvelous ships—absolute 'floating cities'. There was 2,000 passengers and 1,200 crew on those five-day express runs between New York and Southampton and with a quick stop at Cherbourg in each direction. You'd leave Southampton on Thursday and then be in New York on Tuesday. During the trip, there was a special highlight. The *Queen Elizabeth* was specially routed on her way to New York so that she would pass within a quarter-of-a-mile to the *Queen Mary*. It was daylight and both ships looked radiant in the bright sunlight. Each ship was doing some 30 knots and so it was a combined 60-knot encounter that altogether lasted less than five minutes. Two 'monsters' were passing—passing in their reverse relays. The whistles sounded and were deafening. There was cheering. Cameras were going like mad. The Commodore and other officers were on the bridge. It was a great day for Great Britain, for Cunard, for all ocean liners!

'Getting there was half the fun' aboard Cunard in the 1950s. (*Author's Collection*)

Cunard had the largest passenger ship fleet on the Atlantic in the 1950s and carried one-third of all passengers. (*Author's Collection*)

The grand *Queen Mary*, one of the most popular liners of all time. (*Philippe Brebant Collection*)

The 83,673-grt *Queen Elizabeth*, the largest liner afloat in the 1950s and '60s, seen at Cherbourg. (*Author's Collection*)

ORCHESTRAL SELECTIONS
DIRECTED BY JACK GELLER.
Violin Lead - - Jack Davis.

At 11-00 a.m.

o Doble	"ESPANOLA"	Winkler
ction	"GLAMOROUS NIGHTS"	Novello
tz	"LOVE'S LAST WORD IS SPOKEN"	Bixio
r'acte	"COMEDIAN'S GALOP"	Kabalevsky
enade	"NEAPOLITAN"	Winkler
ature	"CAREFREE"	Geller

At 4-45 p.m.

o Doble	"LADY OF MADRID"	Evans
ction	"IM CHAMBRE SEPAREE"	Henberger
tz	"MAID OF THE MOUNTAINS"	Simpson
lo Solo	"PHANTOM MELODY"	Ketelby
(by Fred Baines)		
criptive	"BLACK EYES"	Traditional
ature	"CAREFREE"	Geller

MEAL HOURS

REAKFAST	1st Sitting 8-00 a.m.	2nd Sitting	9-00 a.m.
UNCHEON	" 12-15 p.m.		1-30 p.m.
DINNER	" 6-30 p.m.	"	7-45 p.m.

BAGGAGE

Several Passengers are being inconvenienced by Missing Baggage. Will Passengers please check their baggage and inform the Bedroom Steward or Stewardess of any piece which does not belong in their Cabin.

R.M.S. "SAMARIA"

PROGRAMME OF EVENTS
(Subject to Alteration)

WEDNESDAY, 21st JUNE, 1950

8-00 a.m.	Deck Games available	Sports' Deck
10-00 a.m.	Passenger Boat Drill (Life Jackets to be worn) Passengers are earnestly requested to attend this Drill	
11-00 a.m.	Orchestral Selections	Main Lounge
4-00 p.m.	Afternoon Tea Served on Deck, in Public Rooms and "D" Deck Dining Rooms (Forward & Aft)	
4-30 p.m.	Cinema Cinema Hall, "D" Deck For'd "JOHNNY BELINDA" Featuring :—Jane Wyman, Lew Ayres and Charles Bickford Repeat Performances at 8-30 to-night and to-morrow at 9-45 a.m., 1-30 & 4-30 p.m.	
4-45 p.m.	Tea Time Music	Main Lounge
6-00 p.m.	Cocktail Hour	Star'd Garden Lounge
8-30 p.m.	Cinema Cinema Hall, "D" Deck For'd REPEAT PERFORMANCE	
9-00 p.m.	Horse Racing	Main Lounge
10-00 p.m.	Dancing Port Garden Lounge, Prom. Deck (Weather Permitting)	

FORM B 89.   TOURIST THIRD C

CUNARD LINE
NEW YORK - HAVRE SERVIC

DISEMBARKATION CARD

No. on List *208*.

S.S. SCYTHIA sailing 18 SEP 192?

Mr. *Percy H. Davies*

Ticket No. *777423*

TO BE PRESENTED TO THE IMMIGRATION OFFICER IN EXCHANGE FOR A LANDING CARD

19/9317

Above left: Ship's program aboard Cunard's *Samaria*, June 1950. (*Author's Collection*)

Above right: Disembarkation card from another Cunarder, the *Scythia*. (*Author's Collection*)

Below left: The first commercial jets flew the Atlantic in October 1958 and changed ocean liner history. (*Author's Collection*)

I returned to England several years later, but aboard the *Queen Mary*. It was a rough crossing, but still a pleasant experience. It was all very punctual. We departed from New York on a Wednesday afternoon and then arrived at Southampton on Monday. After that five-night passage, tugs nudged the three-stack *Queen Mary* into the Ocean Terminal. After collecting luggage, I went up to London on the famed, but now long gone, Boat Train to Waterloo Station.

The late Douglass Campbell was a world-class traveler, favoring both passenger trains as well as the great liners. Alone, he could count eight trips aboard the *Queen Mary*, beginning in December 1947. 'There were no stabilizers back then and even a ship as large as the *Queen Mary* rolled tremendously,' he recalled.

The waiters used to soak the tablecloths just to keep the dishes from sliding off the dining room tables. First class was not just luxurious, but very luxurious in those days on the *Queen Mary* and the *Queen Elizabeth*. It was always black tie for dinner. There was a steward as well as stewardess for every first class stateroom. Every piece of your clothing was laid out and your shoes were always polished. The big, oversized bathtubs had four knobs—two for saltwater, two for fresh. The young boys with pillbox hats delivered lots of messages since the inter-cabin phone system was limited. There was no ship-to-shore phone calls, but wireless for long-distance messages. The food was extremely good, lots of roasts and birds, very English, far better than almost anything in London and was always beautifully served. The menus were very extensive, but, of course, you paid extra for the select Verandah Grill.

American Export Lines & United States Lines

Before the Second World War, passenger liner services between New York and the Mediterranean—no matter how opulent or well publicized—never quite had the cachet, the following, or even the high profitability of the Northern ships, in particular those liners sailing to England, France, and Germany. Beginning in the early 1950s, however, the 'Sunny Southern Route,' as it was called, prospered—with celebrities, businessmen, the clergy, tourists, and a brisk post-war wave of westbound immigrants. It was largely in the hands of two companies, the American Export Lines and the Italian Line.

The New York-based American firm had two splendid new liners—the 29,500-ton *Independence* and *Constitution*. As built, they carried 1,000 passengers each in three classes, and were the height of Yankee engineering and modernity. The 683-foot-long liners were the first fully air-conditioned big liners ever. Every cabin, even down in less pricey tourist class, was comfortably air-cooled. With easy conversion to high-capacity troopships should another war arise, the pair was commissioned in 1951. Later, in 1960, they were joined by a third liner, the far smaller, 18,000-ton *Atlantic*, a converted freighter.

The hard-pressed state of the post-war years—a shortage of shipyard berths, a shortage of materials and, in many cases, a shortage of money—prompted more conservative thinking in many steamship line boardrooms. Medium-sized passenger liners were, in many instances, the order of the day. In some instances, aid from the United States, in the form of the post-war Marshall Plan, helped to encourage and support plans for new tonnage. No one planned or could afford big liners similar to those built in the buoyant times of the late 1920s and during the 1930s, extraordinary super ships such as the *Bremen* and *Europa*, the *Rex* and *Conte di Savoia*, the *Normandie* and the *Queen Mary* and *Queen Elizabeth*. No one except the Americans. They actually thought of a combination design—a fast ocean liner for peacetime service, but which could easily become a high-capacity troopship in case of war. Fueled by a possible Soviet push into Europe, there were those in Washington that believed World War III was on the horizon. Ironically, the Americans had a very small share of liner travel in the pre-war years. Now, they would build the most outstanding liner of her time, and one of the most important ships of all time.

Arriving in the high-spirited wake of the 29,500-ton sister ships *Independence* and *Constitution*, was a new Yankee super ship. The 53,300-ton *United States* was commissioned in the summer of 1952. She was, without question, the most brilliant ocean liner of all time, and a tour de force of post-war American design, construction and engineering. On her maiden crossing, departing from Manhattan's Pier 86 on 3 July 1952, she swept the Atlantic, becoming the last liner to capture the coveted Blue Riband for record-breaking speed with an impressive 36 knots. She far outstepped Britain's *Queen Mary* with a record of 31 knots dating from the late 1930s. More importantly, the 990-foot-long US flagship had machinery which, during her otherwise 'top secret' sea trials, produced a near incredible 43 knots. An engineer aboard once told the author, 'She was never quite pushed to the maximum. I am quite sure we could have reached 50 knots!'

The *United States*, carrying up to 1,928 passengers in three classes, sailed between New York, Southampton, Le Havre, and often beyond to Bremerhaven. On her maiden voyage, she crossed in just over three days. Her normal schedule was somewhat less hurried—five days to the Channel ports and six days to Germany. She sailed mostly in Atlantic service for seventeen years, until decommissioned in November 1969. She was immensely popular. In her first ten years, she sailed with a 95 per cent occupancy rate.

The steam turbine, quadruple-screw liner strongly hinted of the 1950s moderne. She had a long, rather low profile that was capped by two enormous funnels, appropriately painted in red, white, and blue. She was, as one author pointed out, the very last liner to accurately embody the concept of a 'sea-going greyhound'. And because of the Cold War, she was also a ship veiled in serious US Government secrecy.

In *The Sway of the Grand Saloon*, the late John Malcolm Brinnin wrote, 'Laid down in a special drydock in 1950, the *United States* was constructed, in secrecy, to blueprints approved by the US Navy and then constructed under the surveillance of Navy personnel.'

Italian Line

The Genoa-headquartered Italians had three well-known pre-war passenger liners, the *Saturnia*, *Vulcania*, and *Conte Biancamano*, and then a succession of newly built, extremely modern liners—the *Andrea Doria* and *Cristoforo Colombo*, the *Augustus* and *Giulio Cesare*, the *Leonardo da Vinci*, and finally the biggest, fastest Mediterranean liner of the time, the 45,900-ton 1,775-passenger sisters *Michelangelo* and *Raffaello*.

By the mid-1970s, they would be all gone—victims of overwhelming operational costs, declining revenues and, most of all, devastating airline competition. In 1976, the struggling *Leonardo da Vinci* made the last New York–Italy passage.

The late Lewis and Ruth Gordon were frequent passengers on Mediterranean crossings in the 1950s and '60s and recalled many of the ships:

One of the great liner sensations of the 1950s, the 29,500-ton *Constitution* takes a turn in dry dock at Baltimore. (*James McNamara Collection*)

Above: New York's Luxury Liner Row was very busy even in the wintery off-season. Seen in this view dated December 1957, from top to bottom, are nine liners: *Berlin, Ocean Monarch, Media, Queen Elizabeth, Liberté, United States, America, Giulio Cesare,* and *Constitution.* (*Author's Collection*)

Right: Advertising for the delights of a crossing. (*Author's Collection*)

Sea Island Club *and First Class Pool,* s. s. INDEPENDENCE *and* s. s. CONSTITUTION.

With the *Berlin* just arriving on the left, another winter scene along the New York City waterfront—this one dated January 1960—with (from top to bottom) seven other liners at berth: *Homeric, Gripsholm, Ocean Monarch, Mauretania, Liberté, Constitution,* and *Saturnia.* (*Author's Collection*)

QUADRUPL̲E̲ ̲ ̲ ̲ ̲ TURBINE STE̲A̲MSHIP
"UNIT̲E̲D̲ STATES"
COMMODORE JOHN W. ANDERSON
Captain, U. S. N. R.

Abstract of Log

From SOUTHAMPTON to NEW YORK,

Left **Nab Tower,** 2:53 p.m., BST, Aug. 16, 1957   Arrived **Havre L. V.,** , Aug. 16, 19

Distance, Nab Tower to Le Havre L. V.: 75 Miles

Steaming Time: 2 Hours, 50 Minutes — Average Speed. 26.47 Knots

DATE	LAT. N.	LONG. W.	NAUT. MILES	SPEED	WIND	REMARKS
Aug. 17						Departure Havre L. V., 1:34 a.m., BST.
Aug. 17	49-51	8-16	320	30.68	NW-5	Moderate sea. Moderate NW'ly swell.
Aug. 18	48-41	28-26	790	31.29	WSW-4	Slight sea. Low WSW'ly swell.
Aug. 19	44-12	46-27	790	31.29	Var.-6-3	Slight sea. Low WSW'ly swell.
Aug. 20	41-24	63-26	777	30.77	NE-4	Moderate sea. Low E'ly swell.
Aug. 21			478	26.26	NW-3	Arrived Ambrose L. V., 4:57 a.m., EDT.

Total Distance, Le Havre to New York: 3,1

Steaming Time: 4 Days, 8 Hours, 23 Minutes — Average . Knots

NOTE: A Nautical Mile is approximately 15 per cent longer than a Statute or Land Mile

Above left: The brilliant *United States* being berthed in an icy Hudson River. (*United States Lines*)

Above right: Voyage log dated 16 August 1957. (*Author's Collection*)

Right: High dining: A section of the first class dining room aboard the *United States*. (*United States Lines*)

Economy with comfort: An inside three-berth room in tourist class priced from $175 per person for five days in the late 1950s. (*United States Lines*)

Midnight sailing: The glowing *United States* prepares for another crossing to New York. (*United States Lines*)

Above left: Actress Deborah Kerr returning from England aboard the *Queen Mary* in 1949. (*Author's Collection*)

Above right: Bound for a summer in Europe: a young lady poses before setting sail aboard the *United States* in July 1955. (*Author's Collection*)

Left: Four young German ladies represent the four passenger ships of the otherwise short-lived Arosa Line in a photo dated 1957. (*Author's Collection*)

Above: Families, friends and well-wishers greet the liner *America* at New York in 1950. (*United States Lines*)

Left: Bon voyage! Farewell to passengers aboard Sweden's *Kungsholm* in a photo dated 1955. (*Author's Collection*)

Above left: In July 1952, France's brand new *Flandre* broke down on her maiden crossing to New York and had to be towed into port. (*James McNamara Collection*)

Above right: When Sweden's 23,500-ton *Gripsholm* arrived in New York for the first time, in May 1957, it was said to be the beginning of a new generation of Atlantic liners. (*Moran Towing & Transportation Co.*)

Right: Halifax, Nova Scotia, was an alternative to New York for landing North America-bound passengers. Here West Germany's *Berlin* is arriving. (*Halifax Maritime Museum*)

In first class aboard the *Independence* and *Constitution*, it was quite usual to see five and ten carat diamond rings at dinner. But when one woman wore a forty-seven carat diamond, it was called 'vulgar' by the others. There were always Greek shipping magnates onboard. I remember Mrs Goulandris, who wore jewels from the best shops in Paris—and most of them, it seemed, at the same time! Onboard, daily life was actually quiet, even simple. There were some evening activities, like dancing, horse-racing and films, but otherwise you sat on deck all day long with little to do. Reading and writing letters were the great pastimes. In the 1950s, daytime attire in first class was like today's evening clothes.

'We also liked the Italian Line very much,' added Mr Gordon:

The older ships, such as the *Saturnia* and *Vulcania*, which dated from the 1920s, had 'over-the-edge' decor, where enough is not quite enough. They were very, very ornate and very dark in tone. There were first class staterooms on the *Saturnia* and *Vulcania*, and they had their own verandas, then quite a novelty. If you booked these, you rarely had to leave your cabin and never, ever had to go out on the crowded Lido Deck. On the modernized *Conte Biancamano*, the walls of the card and writing rooms were done in exquisite inlaid woods, all themed to card games.

Italian Line also had the best costume balls. There were Renaissance, Gypsy, Baroque and Venetian balls and creations to match. Amazingly, the Italians gave out great prizes for the very costumes they provided.

Italian Line also had the most tearful farewells, especially at ports like Messina and Palermo in Sicily. It was high drama in bidding goodbyes. These farewells sometimes included three generations of a family on the pierside. Very often, these Italian immigrants traveling in tourist class aboard the *Saturnia*, *Vulcania*, and later the *Cristoforo Colombo* were bound for Canada. Many Italian Line crossings stopped at Halifax two or three days before reaching New York.

'We also recall one other special sailing,' concluded the Gordons. 'Each year, one eastbound sailing aboard either American Export or the Italian Line carried New York designers and buyers bound for the Italian fashion shows. That sailing was always known as the "Seventh Avenue Special"!'

A Moran tug assists with the undocking of the 700-foot-long *Cristoforo Colombo* at New York. (*Moran Towing & Transportation Co.*)

Genoa was among the Mediterranean's busiest ports, here showing the *Augustus* on the left and the *Cristoforo Colombo* on the right. (*Richard Faber Collection*)

Carl Evers was a superb marine artist. In this creation, he has captured a Christmas Eve departure of the 27,000-ton *Augustus* from New York in 1957. (*Moran Towing & Transportation Co.*)

Left: Another busy day at Genoa, homeport for the Italian Line. From left to right in this 1960 view are the *Anna "C", Bianca "C", Cabo San Roque, Federico "C"*, and the brand new *Leonardo da Vinci*. (*Paolo Piccione Collection*)

Below: Farewell at Naples from the decks of the *Michelangelo*—and with P&O's *Oronsay* in the distance. (*Maurizio Eliseo Collection*)

Togetherness at Genoa: The stunning 45,900-ton *Michelangelo* on the left; the 33,500-ton *Leonardo da Vinci* to the right. (*Author's Collection*)

The very spacious bedroom and sitting room of a suite aboard the *Michelangelo*. It was priced from $1,500 per person in the mid-1960s for a seven-day crossing to Italy. (*Italian Line*)

The Decline

Speedy jet aircraft began regular trans-Atlantic service in October 1958. It was not only the great divide, but a dramatic one. In six months, the airlines had two-thirds of all trans-ocean passengers; in five years, they had 98 per cent. The era of the traditional passenger ship was all but over—and throughout the world.

Losing a million pounds per year since the early 1960s, the *Queens* were finally retired from service—the thirty-one-year-old *Queen Mary* in September 1967, and the twenty-eight-year-old *Queen Elizabeth* in November 1968. Douglass Campbell made the *Mary's* last Atlantic crossing from New York. He remembered:

> By then, there had been a great cutback in help. There were economies everywhere. Cunard was desperately trying to rekindle the bygone style, but it was really lost glamour, an illusion. John Roosevelt was the auctioneer for the ship's mileage pool and author Walter Lord was aboard. We passed the *Elizabeth* at night and felt very sad. We thought that the onboard model of the *QE2*, then still building, looked so strange, so different.

The *France* proved to be the very last of the great French Line on the North Atlantic run. Time had run out. Even if her passenger loads were declining slightly, it was the 1035-foot-long ship's high operational costs, especially fuel oil, that did her in. By 1973–74, she was receiving $14 million in annual subsidies from the French Ministry of Marine. There was some harsh rethinking and government ministers decided that such subsidy money would be better spent with Air France and its Concorde project. Alone, there was far greater prestige in that extraordinary supersonic aircraft. The *France* was quite abruptly decommissioned in September 1974. Douglass Campbell was aboard some of that very grand ship's final crossings:

> The service was absolutely impeccable and the food outstanding. We dined in the Chambord Restaurant and sometimes at the captain's table, where the service was even better. The *France* had a fantastic wine cellar, probably the best at sea back then. House wines were, of course, complimentary on the French Line. The *France* was a very special ship and especially in first class. Many people knew one another or had friends who knew them. She lost lots of money actually, but was really built for the prestige of France. De Gaulle believed strongly in national status. In the end, in the early 1970s, she was losing a fortune. De Gaulle himself had been her guardian angel, but without him [he died in 1969], the *France* was really finished. She went on to the end in a great, grand style. It was sad to see her go.

Rough seas could be part of an Atlantic crossing—and as seen in this view from aboard the *Rotterdam.* (*Holland America Line*)

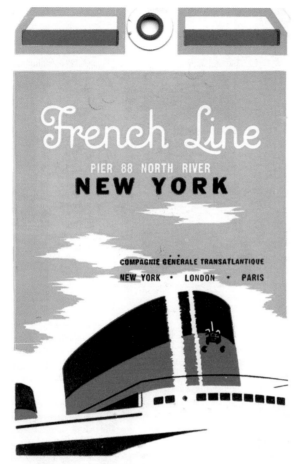

Above left: 'It is good to be on a well-run ship' was the apt slogan of the Holland America Line. (*Author's Collection*)

Middle: French Line was perhaps best noted for its splendid kitchens—'More sea gulls followed the French liners than any others,' it was said in travel circles. (*Author's Collection*)

Above right: The *France* of 1962 was the North Atlantic sensation of her time. (*Author's Collection*)

Pour votre Toutou.... Madame
Pour votre fidèle
Compagnon ... Monsieur

MENU
=

Le Plat de Tayaut
(Consommé de Bœuf - Toasts - Légumes)

Le Régal de Sweekey
(Carottes - Viande Hachée - Epinards - Toasts)

La Gâterie "FRANCE"
(Haricots Verts - Poulet Haché - Riz Nature
Arrosé de Jus de Viande et de Biscottes en Poudre)

La Préférence du Danois
(Os de Côte de Bœuf, de Jambon et de Veau)

Le Régime Végétarien des Dogs
(Tous les Légumes Frais et Toutes les Pâtes Alimentaires)

Biscuit - Ken'l

COMPAGNIE GÉNÉRALE TRANSATLANTIQUE

French Line
PAQUEBOT "FRANCE"

Above: What better way to sail to or from Europe than by ship, 1960. (*Author's Collection*)

Left: Even dogs ate well aboard the splendid *France*. (*Author's Collection*)

Opposite: Evocative art: Night-time passage on Canadian Pacific's famed Empress liners, sailing between Liverpool and Montreal. (*Author's Collection*)

TRAVERSEZ
L'ATLANTIQUE
EN BEAUTÉ
DANS UN
"EMPRESS"
DU
Canadien Pacifique

3

SOUTHERN WATERS:
TO LATIN AMERICA

Royal Mail Lines

One of the best known liner routes to South America was aboard Britain's Royal Mail Lines. 'At Royal Mail, you were trained as a steward as if in a Russian ballet school,' recalled the late Ron Peach, who served aboard no less than five Royal Mail passenger ships—the *Alcantara, Andes, Highland Monarch, Amazon,* and *Aragon.* Their trade, back in the 1950s and '60s, was the UK–East Coast of South America run, from either Southampton or London via Vigo (in Spain), Lisbon, and Las Palmas (in the Canary Islands) across the mid-Atlantic to Rio de Janeiro, Santos, Montevideo, and Buenos Aires. London to Buenos Aires took nearly three weeks on what was probably the finest ocean liner service to Latin America in its day.

Ron Peach served in first class aboard Royal Mail's otherwise three-class ships—with first, cabin, and tourist class accommodations:

You served full afternoon tea in the staterooms and suites, for example, and then returned to lay out the evening clothes, which included putting the studs in a gentlemen's dress shirts. Years later, in the early 1970s, when I joined the Cunard Line and the *Queen Elizabeth 2,* it seemed much more informal by comparison to first class on Royal Mail Lines.

After the Second World War, Royal Mail restarted their South American passenger service with the 25,000-ton *Andes,* built in 1939,

and the rebuilt *Alcantara,* a 22,000-ton liner constructed in 1926. They were the company's prime ships, based at Southampton, and for a time the 669-foot-long *Andes* was both the largest and most luxurious liner on the run between Europe and South America. Royal Mail also ran a separate passenger as well as a cargo service out of London, using the 1929–30 built 'Highland boats' as they were called—the *Highland Monarch, Highland Chieftain, Highland Brigade,* and *Highland Princess*—which were a series of motor ships, noted by their very squat stacks and split, separate superstructures. Royal Mail actually added a new combination passenger-cargo liner, the *Magdalena,* in 1949, but she was wrecked and lost on no less than her maiden voyage.

Ron Peach continues:

In the 1950s, the Argentine passengers going up to England in first class on Royal Mail were all multi-millionaires, born in Argentina but with British educations, tastes and manners. Often, they owned huge, 100,000-acre estancias [ranches] in Argentina, but also maintained homes in London as well as Paris and in the English countryside. Some of them also owned half the beef that was in the ship's refrigerated cargo holds.

It was completely top-drawer in those days on Royal Mail. You were never, ever known by your Christian name, but simply as Peach. You were much like a butler in some grand house. It was all silver service in the restaurant. In fact, you could hardly lift the silver trays because they were so heavy. The food was, of course, beyond compare. There were great platters of meat and veg. We used to ring bells as a call for dinner aboard the *Alcantara* and *Andes*.

While the *Alcantara* sailed off to a Japanese scrapyard in 1958, the *Andes* was soon converted for full-time cruising, catering to a very select 500 passengers in all first-class configuration.

The South American service continued for another decade, until 1968–69, but had been entrusted by then to a brand new trio of handsome-looking passenger-cargo liners, the 20,000-ton *Amazon* and her twin sisters, *Aragon* and *Arlanza*. Capped by single, buff yellow-colored funnels, they were in fact the last passenger ships in the British fleet to have 'split' superstructures (the officers being separated from the passenger-guests) and the very last to carry three classes: first, cabin, and third class. They were, however, somewhat late for the South American passenger run, which was typically being overtaken by the airlines in the 1960s and all while the cargo side of their operations were complicated by more and more strikes, and often in the port of London. 'These ships sometimes returned to South America with the same cargo that they had brought north on the previous trip,' noted Ron Peach. 'The London dockers had been on yet another long strike and refused to unload ships such as these. Royal Mail was not only beginning to lose patience, but lots of money as well.'

These days, Royal Mail is no more, having been more fully integrated into Britain's Furness Withy shipping group, which was later sold off to the Chinese and then to the Germans. Most recently, Furness Withy's remaining shipping interests were a part of Hamburg-Sud, the Hamburg-South American Line. Earlier, by 1969, the *Amazon* and her two sisters were sold off, going to the Shaw Savill Line for a very short, very unsuccessful time (Shaw Savill was also part of the Furness Withy family) before being sold and totally rebuilt for the Norwegians as bulky auto-carriers. The grand old *Andes* proved to be the last of the Royal Mail passenger liners. She ran her final cruise out of Southampton in April 1971, and then made a short hop across the Channel to Belgium, where she was broken-up. Later, as a reminder of those stylish ocean liner days, Royal Mail operated a containership on the UK–South America run. Sentimentally, she was named *Andes*.

Blue Star Line

Another route to South America was aboard the one-class, almost yacht-like passenger-cargo ships of the London-based Blue Star Line. London-born John Spooner recalled his time working for Blue Star Line:

I served as a deckhand with the Blue Star Line, which ran four combination passenger-cargo liners down to South America from London. I served on three of them—the *Argentina Star, Paraguay Star* and *Uruguay Star*. Somehow, I missed the fourth, the *Brasil Star*. The ships were known as the 'BA Flyers'. They could make the run from London to Buenos Aires in two-and-a-half weeks. Otherwise, the full round trips took seven weeks. These ships were very crisply run, catering to a business trade and some high-end travelers and tourists. They had very smart interiors for only fifty passengers each. They were very much like smart London clubs but at sea. Blue Star was owned by the very rich Vestey family and they use to personally inspect these ships during their layovers in the London Docks. Everything had to shine and gleam. Once, I told Lord Vestey to 'clear off'. It was a mistake, of course—I didn't recognize him!

The Vestey family owned hundreds of butcher shops throughout the UK as well as Armour and Swift meat companies. They also had vast holdings in South America, especially in Argentina. And of course they owned Blue Star, which altogether had about fifty or sixty ships back then. We used to load huge quantities of beef carcasses at Buenos Aires. It was chilled, however, and not frozen—and hung on hooks. I remember we used to clean those hooks with something called Topane, which burned your hands. The cargo holds were cavernous and the meat compartments had big, insulated doors. At night, when the day's loading was complete, we'd go ashore. Buenos Aires was a great place. You got a steak dinner for as little as 50 cents!

George Pilgrim recalled:

Going to sea was an adventure, especially for a young man in still-ravaged Britain, back in the 1950s. I signed on with the Blue Star Line. I was hired from a pool, from where you were sent to different

Above: The 14,000-ton *Highland Brigade* and her sisters looked after Royal Mail's South American run from London. (*Richard Faber Collection*)

Left: Royal Mail Lines' *Alcantara* and *Asturias* were the sensational British sisters on the South American run in the 1930s. But after the War, the *Asturias* was retained as a British troop transport and is seen here returning to Southampton in September 1953. (*Cronican-Arroyo Collection*)

Below: Combined services to all of South America: Royal Mail Lines to the East Coast and Pacific Line to the West. (*Author's Collection*)

CRUISES..
ROUND
VOYAGES..

Expect something quite, quite different when you

sail

WITH

ROYAL MAIL

OR

PACIFIC LINE

Not just a voyage
but a fascinating
experience

All-Year-Round Cruises

'ANDES' 27,000 tons

From Southampton to the Orient, West Indes and Mediterranean. 'ANDES' is a beautiful ship, comfortable, air-conditioned and stabilised Every cabin has its own bath or shower, and private toilet. The restaurant accommodates all passengers at one sitting.

ROUND VOYAGES

'AMAZON' 'ARAGON' 'ARLANZA' 20,000 tons

Round voyages by modern air-conditioned, stabilised passenger ners to Brazi, Uruguay, Argentina, via France, Spain, Portugal and Canary Isles. First-class, cabin-class and third-class accommodation.

'REINA DEL'MAR' 20,000 tons
FLAGSHIP OF THE PACIFIC LINE

Special 64-day Winter Round Voyage Liverpool to France, Spain, Portugal, Florida, Nassau, Jamaica Panama Cana, Peru and Ch le Ar-conditioned—stabilised, with spacious decks for games and relaxation, swimming pools, cinemascope and shopping arcades, and famed for excellent cuis ne.

ROYAL MAIL LINES LIMITED
THE PACIFIC STEAM NAVIGATION COMPANY

BOOK THROUGH WAKEFIELD FORTUNE LIMITED

Page Three

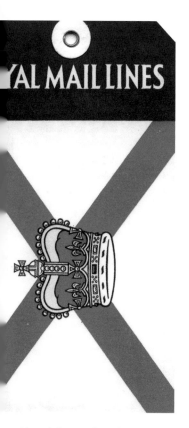

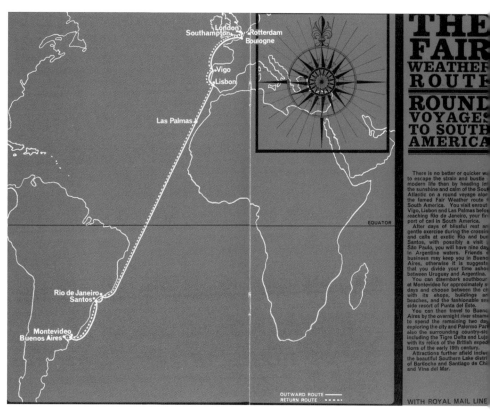

Above left: Royal Mail Lines was a very popular run to South America well into the 1950s. (*Author's Collection*)

Middle The *Amazon, Aragon,* and *Arlanza* were the new additions to the South American liner run in 1959–60. (*Author's Collection*)

Above right: Sailing to Brazil and Argentina, to the South Atlantic, was dubbed 'the fair weather route'. (*Author's Collection*)

BLUE STAR LINE
accommodation plans

Argentina Star
Brasil Star
Paraguay Star
Uruguay Star

Above: London-based Blue Star Line ran four very fine combo liners
on the UK–South America run. (*Author's Collection*)

Right: Winter sunshine voyages were heavily promoted as idyllic escapes
from the cold, dark English winters. (*Author's Collection*)

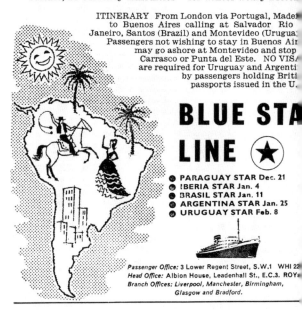

WINTER VOYAGES
to fabulous
SOUTH AMERICA b
BLUE STAR

THESE are *exclusively first-class* passages which guarant
sun, interest, entertainment, superb accommodation a
cuisine, no currency difficulties   for winter weary Britor

ITINERARY From London via Portugal, Made
to Buenos Aires calling at Salvador Rio
Janeiro, Santos (Brazil) and Montevideo (Urugua
Passengers not wishing to stay in Buenos Air
may go ashore at Montevideo and stop
Carrasco or Punta del Este. NO VISA
are required for Uruguay and Argenti
by passengers holding Briti
passports issued in the U.

**BLUE STA
LINE** ⭐

PARAGUAY STAR Dec. 21
IBERIA STAR Jan. 4
BRASIL STAR Jan. 11
ARGENTINA STAR Jan. 25
URUGUAY STAR Feb. 8

Passenger Office: 3 Lower Regent Street, S.W.1 WHI 22
Head Office: Albion House, Leadenhall St., E.C.3. ROYa
Branch Offices: Liverpool, Manchester, Birmingham,
Glasgow and Bradford.

shipping companies. I was assigned to the *Argentina Star* as a cook and baker. She carried only fifty all-first class passengers and so was like some cozy, sea-going club. The run from London down to Buenos Aires took, as I remember, almost three weeks. We'd call on the way at Lisbon, Las Palmas, Rio, Santos, and Montevideo. Then at Buenos Aires, we'd stay for as long as two weeks, mostly to load the Argentine beef that being shipped to the UK, before reversing course and heading home.

Pacific Steam Navigation Co. Ltd

Another long-established British liner company involved in Latin America service was the Pacific Steam Navigation Company Limited, PSNC for short. Their fleet was headed by two, very well-known liners—the *Reina Del Pacifico*, built in 1931, and her eventual replacement, the 1956-constructed *Reina Del Mar*. Their routing was quite extensive, on very port-filled itineraries. From Liverpool, the routing was La Rochelle, Santander and Corunna before crossing to Bermuda, Nassau, Havana, Kingston, La Guaira, Curacao, Cartagena, Cristobal, La Libertad, Callao, Arica, Antofagasta, and turnaround at Valparasio. 'We had lots of colonial-type passengers on the West Coast of South America run of the *Reina Del Pacifico* and *Reina Del Mar*, plus lots of businessmen,' recalled John Jones. 'It was still three-class and I recall that first class was really too quiet, even too dull, and so these rich, well-dressed passengers would often march down to more casual, fun-filled tourist class in the evenings.' While the aged *Reina Del Pacifico* went to the breakers in 1958, the *Reina Del Mar* had a service life of only seven years, until 1963, when she was sold off to serve in a more viable role: as a full-time cruise ship.

Booth Line

Another British shipowner, the Booth Line maintained an unusual service—across the mid-Atlantic from Liverpool to the Caribbean and then 1,000 miles up to the Amazon River to Manaus. John Jones sailed aboard that company's passenger ships: the *Hilary*, *Hildebrand*, and *Hubert*.

These voyages along the Amazon were hot, steamy, thickly humid. The crew would often sleep on deck. Below, if you opened a porthole, insects of all sizes and types would come flooding in! The ships' navigating officers had to be very careful because of submerged rocks and floating logs in the river. Once, we bent the ship's only screw and then limped to Manaus. There was no shipyard in such a remote place and so two Brazilian divers were hired to make repairs. They carved away some of the twisted steel which actually made the ship faster than before. The chief engineer was more than surprised—and pleased! We carried businessmen, traders and sometimes even a few tourists in first class, and missionaries, medical people and teachers in tourist class. The crew often bought parrots and birds in Manaus and then brought them home to Liverpool. Myself, I bought a little Cayman, kept it in my cabin, but then discovered it didn't like colder climates. Soon after landing in Liverpool, I gave it to the Chester Zoo. Liverpool customs were easy in those days. Give them a few pounds and almost anything could be brought in!

Fyffes Line

British, Elders & Fyffes were noted for their 'banana boat' passenger liner, as well as cargo services to the Caribbean. John Williams worked on the Southampton Docks some sixty years ago, back in the 1950s. We met for a breakfast chat onboard a recent *Queen Mary 2* voyage:

Yes, I remember working most of the great liners—Cunard, Union-Castle, P&O, and the short calls of the European ships like the *Nieuw Amsterdam*, *Ile de France* and *Bremen*. I thought the *Nieuw Amsterdam* was among the most beautiful liners and I also gave high marks to the good lines of ships such as the *Andes* and *Caronia*. We had lots of other, smaller ships too. It was always a thrill to deal with the Elders & Fyffes banana boats for obvious reasons. These were beautiful ships sometimes carrying as many as 100 passengers and with names such as *Camito* and *Golfito*. We used to be given bunches of green bananas brought over from the Caribbean. We'd take them home and let them slowly ripen. They'd often last until the next Fyffes boat arrived. Luckily for me, no big spiders ever emerged from them.

The 20,000-ton, three-class *Reina Del Mar*, commissioned in 1956, was the finest liner on the West Coast of South America run. (*Roger Sherlock*)

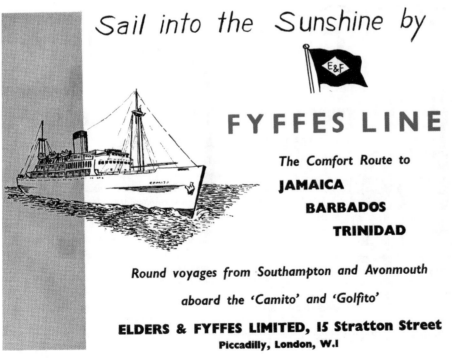

Sail into the Sunshine by

E&F

FYFFES LINE

The Comfort Route to

JAMAICA

BARBADOS

TRINIDAD

Round voyages from Southampton and Avonmouth

aboard the 'Camito' and 'Golfito'

ELDERS & FYFFES LIMITED, 15 Stratton Street
Piccadilly, London, W.I

BOOK THROUGH WAKEFIELD FORTUNE LIMITED   *Page Thirty Three*

Fyffes Line to the sunny Caribbean was especially popular in winter. (*Author's Collection*)

Italian Line

Two of the finest liners on the Europe–South America run were the handsome-looking Italian liners *Augustus* and *Giulio Cesare*. They gave long and popular service, having traded to the ports of the South American East Coast for over twenty years.

Captain Lorenzo Calvillo also sailed on some of the great Italian liners on the South American run—the *Conte Biancamano, Conte Grande, Augustus* and *Giulio Cesare*, during the 1950s. 'In first class,' the Captain recalled, 'we had wealthy businessmen, the high Catholic clergy and some migrants who had prospered in South America but who were returning to Europe for a visit. Some very wealthy passengers took inter-connecting suites. Occasionally, we'd have royalty as well, who would sail with personal servants, lots of luggage and special cases filled with jewelry.'

Captain Calvillo sailed mostly to the East Coast of South America, to Rio de Janeiro, Santos, Montevideo, and Buenos Aires, but he also made a trip to the West Coast, to Guayaquil, Callao, and Valparaiso, aboard the *Paolo Toscanelli*:

The *Toscanelli* was a 9,000-ton ship, carrying cargo mostly, but also about 125 passengers in first class and 500 in third class, which was actually a kind of steerage for that time. The Italian immigrants going to South America used to sleep in the 'tween decks around all the cargo holds. The men and women were separated. As a young officer then, I was on patrol. It was very, very hot—only forced-air ventilation. All of these third class passengers were very poor and altogether were quite grateful to be moving to countries such as Argentina, Brazil, Venezuela, Peru and Chile. In those times, South America was like 'El Dorado,' the promised land. Italians went there to farm, to open restaurants, to start small businesses. In fact, there was a suburb of Buenos Aires where people spoke Italian, but with a Genovese dialect.

Grimaldi-Siosa Lines

In her final years, in the 1970s, the Italian liner *Irpinia* had renewed popularity. She sailed as a Mediterranean cruise ship and on itineraries that were often linked to the European tours of Pan American Airways. The *Irpinia* had a long career, including long stints in Latin American service as a migrant ship and—near the end of her days—a starring role in a major motion picture, *Voyage of the Damned*.

Owned by the Genoa-based Grimaldi-Siosa Lines, their early fleet consisted of second-hand, largely rebuilt ships that were generally aimed at the low-fare markets. The 13,204-grt *Irpinia* was the company flagship for some years. Originally built in 1929 at Newcastle in England, she was first owned by the French, belonging to Marseilles-headquartered Transports Maritimes. She was then named *Campana* and sailed out of Marseilles to the East Coast of South America—to Rio, Santos, Montevideo, and Buenos Aires.

After the fall of France to Nazi invaders in 1940, she was laid-up at Buenos Aires and later seized by the Argentines. For a time thereafter, she sailed as their *Rio Jachal*. But in 1946, with the War over, she was returned to French, was renamed *Campana*, and again traded on the Europe–South America run as well as on voyages to colonial Indochina. She was sold to Grimaldi-Siosa in 1955 and renamed *Irpinia*. She was rebuilt at a Genoa shipyard, being given a new, more modern raked bow in the process. Her original three-class quarters were rearranged to take 187 in first class and 1,034 in tourist.

She sailed initially between Italy and the West Indies, carrying migrants mostly and often to new lives in Venezuela. In 1959–60, she spent two summers on a more northern route, sailing between the Mediterranean, Quebec City, and Montreal. She also made periodic trips to New York. 'We carried mostly Hungarian immigrants to Canada,' remembered Ugo Frangini, the ship's one-time chief purser. 'The *Irpinia* was actually chartered to a relief organization that brought these immigrants through Austria to the ports of Genoa and Naples.'

In 1962, the 537-foot-long liner had another facelift. This time, her twin funnels were replaced by a single tapered stack, new Fiat diesels replaced her original steam turbines and her passenger quarters were again modernized. Hereafter, she returned to a busy, very profitable, uniquely 'double' migrant service. She was routed between Southampton, Corunna, Vigo, and Madeira, and then across to Barbados, Trinidad, La Guaira, Curacao, Kingston, Ciudad Trujillo, St Kitts, Montserrat, and Antigua. Return passages were to Lisbon, Vigo, and Southampton. She took thousands of Spanish and Portuguese migrants (and sometimes workers) westbound, and then West Indian migrants (mostly Jamaicans) bound for Britain on the

Left: Genoa was a popular port for liner services to South America. Here (from left to right) are Italy's *Conte Grande*, Spain's *Cabo de Hornos*, and two other Italian liners, the *Sebastiano Caboto* and, just departing, the *Conte Biancamano*. (*Richard Faber Collection*)

Below left: A four-berth cabin in tourist class aboard the *Conte Biancamano* in 1949. (*Italian Line*)

Below right: Third class dining area aboard the *Conte Biancamano*. (*Italian Line*)

Above: Italian Line was well known for the passing of its ships at sea. Both on the Italy–South America run, the *Augustus* (left) closely passes her sister *Giulio Cesare* (right). (*Author's Collection*)

Right: Festive advertising promoting Italian Line's 'Sunny Southern Route'. (*Author's Collection*)

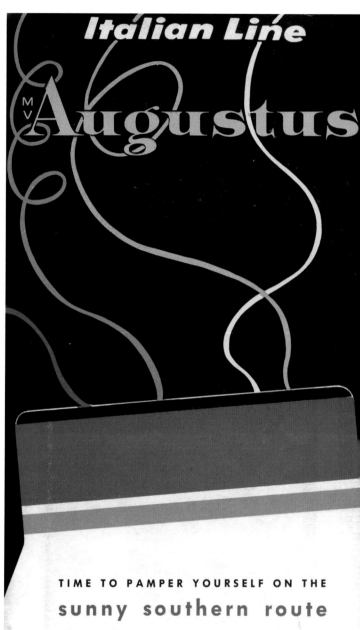

Above: In her final years, the 1951-built *Augustus* served as a floating hotel and entertainment center berthed in Manila. She had been renamed *Philippines* by then. (*Peter Knego Collection*)

Right: Sailing to the far-off West Indies aboard the Italian *Irpinia*. (*Author's Collection*)

EUROPE
WEST INDIES - JAMAICA
EUROPE
LINE

ITINERARY
& TARIFFS
EDITION
N° 5
July 1966

MOTORVESSEL
IRPINIA
1966-1967

SIOSA
line

A sailing schedule for the Europe–Caribbean services of the 13,200-ton *Irpinia*. (*Author's Collection*)

RARY 1966–1967   M/v IRPINIA

EUROPE   WEST INDIES – JAMAICA – EUROPE Line   from **EUROPE** to

Passage fares per adult

DECKS	Cabin Number	Cabin Type		when occupied by	WEST INDIES and viceversa	LA GUAIRA CURAÇAO
					POUNDS STERLING	
TOURIST CLASS "B"		SIXBERTH		6 pers.	75	92
		FOURBERTH		4	80	94
		TWOBERTH		2	85	100
TOURIST CLASS "A"		FOURBERTH		4 pers.	90	98
		TWOBERTH		2	95	109
		FOURBERTH, Inside shower / toilet		4	95	111
		FOURBERTH, Outside, shower / toilet		4	100	111
		TWOBERTH, Inside shower / toilet		2	105	121
		TWOBERTH, Outside shower / toilet		2	110	121
FIRST CLASS	302-304-310 314-317-320	FOURBERTH, Outside		4 pers.	118	125
MAIN	307	THREEBERTH, Outside		3	123	134
	301 312 318 319	TWOBERTH, Outside		2	123	134
	300 303 311 323	TWOBERTH, Outside		2	123	134
	305 306 308 309 315 316 321 322	TWOBERTH, Outside, shower and toilet		2	146	161
PROMENADE	218 223	FOURBERTH, Inside, shower & toilet		4 pers.	131	143
	211 - 212 216 - 217	FOURBERTH, Outside	without shower & toilet	4 / 3	123 / 131	143 / 143
			with shower & toilet	4 / 3	139 / 146	152 / 161
	N	THREEBERTH, Outside		3 / 2	131 / 146	143 / 161
	C E H J 201 202	THREEBERTH, Outside	without bath & toilet	3 / 2	131 / 146	143 / 161
			with bath & toilet	3 / 2	146 / 169	161 / 188
	205 206 209 210	THREEBERTH, Outside, shower and toilet		3 / 2	146 / 169	161 / 188
	M	TWOBERTH, Outside		2	131	143
	219 220 221	TWOBERTH, Inside, shower and toilet		2	146	161
	D F I 203 - 204	TWOBERTH, Outside	without bath & toilet	2	131	143
			with bath & toilet	2	154	170
	G	TWOBERTH, Outside, bath & toilet		2	154	170
	L	SINGLE, Outside	without bath and toilet	1	154	170
			with bath and toilet	1	184	205
LIDO	106 107 108	FOURBERTH, Inside, shower & toilet		4 pers. / 2 / 1	139 / 152 / 161	152 / 170 / 179
	111 114	TWOBERTH, Outside		2 / 1	152 / 161	170 / 179
	103 105	TWOBERTH, Inside, shower & toilet		2	154	170
	125 126 129	TWOBERTH, Outside, shower & toilet		2 / 1	161 / 192	179 / 214
	109 110 121 122 130	TWOLOWBED, Outside, shower & toilet		2	176	196
	115-116-119-120	SINGLES, Outside, shower & toilet		1	192	214
	A B	APARTMENTS, Outside, two low beds, bath and toilet		2 / 1	207 / 298	232 / 339
BOAT	1 2	TWOBERTH, Outside, lounge, shower and toilet		2 / 1	176 / 222	196 / 250

In the cabins marked with (●), on request, a sofa can be added at   118   125

FIRST CLASS interchangeable cabins Main and A Decks   Fares on application.

Minimum throughfare { to BRITISH GUIANA £ 85 / from BRITISH GUIANA £ 80 }

FOR ALL THOSE VOYAGES WHEN SOUTHAMPTON IS NOT CALLED DIRECTLY, PASSENGERS WILL EMBARK OR DEBARK AT GENOA AND TRANSPORTATION FROM / TO LONDON WILL BE AT COMPANY'S EXPENSE.

Vessel calls also at Naples.

EXCURSION FARES: 20% reduction on roundtrips starting in the west Indies between 1/11.66 and 28/2/67; return not later than 60 days from date of landing in Europe.

CRUISE   LA GUAIRA-Departure 21/3/1967—MARTINIQUE 22-23/3 – 23/3-GUADELOUPE 23-24/3–S. KITTS 24/3–S. THOMAS (Vir. Is.) 25/3 – AN P.R. 26-27/3 –CURAÇAO 28/3 – LA GUAIRA Arrival 29/3.

(DATES FARES AND CONDITIONS SHOWN IN THIS TARIFF ARE SUBJECT TO ALTERATION WITHOUT PREVIOUS NOTICE)

The 537-foot-long *Irpinia* on a rare visit to New York in August 1959. (*Moran Towing & Transportation Co.*)

One of the *Irpinia's* fleetmates was the 9,600-ton *Ascania*. (*Author's Collection*)

return trips. The *Irpinia* was often full to capacity on both legs. By 1970, however, she turned mostly to cruising, usually on week-long runs out of Genoa to Cannes, Barcelona, Palma, Tunis, Palermo, and Capri. Her seven-day voyages were priced from $79, and a two-week Christmas cruise to the Canary Islands would cost from $134.

Companhia Colonial

Two other new and important passenger liners trading to Latin America were Portugal's sister ships *Vera Cruz* and *Santa Maria*, commissioned in 1952–53. Based at Lisbon, the *Vera Cruz* sailed to Brazil while the *Santa Maria* traded to Venezuela and the Caribbean. It was the *Santa Maria* that became world famous—she made headlines all over the world, dominating the evening news even on American television for well over a week. . On 22 January 1961, while sailing in West Indian waters, she was hijacked by terrorist rebels. For eleven days, the name of the Portuguese liner *Santa Maria* (at the same time, the US-flag Grace Line had a passenger-cargo ship of the same name and the two sometimes met in the Caribbean) became a household item. The capture of the 609-foot-long *Santa Maria* made history. Several books were later written about this affair.

Owned by Lisbon-headquartered Companhia Colonial, the 20,900-grt *Santa Maria* and her sister were the largest and most luxurious Portuguese-flag liners of their time. While their owners were primarily interested in the colonial trade to Portuguese Africa, to Angola and Mozambique, and the largely migrant trade to Brazil, the 1,078-passenger *Santa Maria* was rather unique in being detoured to a special mid-Atlantic service. Based at Lisbon, she called regularly at Madeira, Teneriffe, La Guaira, Curacao, Havana (later changed to San Juan), and finally Port Everglades, Florida, then a small, developing port. Her trade was generally transporting migrants to Venezuela and other general passenger traffic. She had a very fine first class for 156 travelers, a less spacious, less ornate cabin class for 226, and then a large, but rather basic third class for nearly 700. Built at Hoboken in Belgium, the 20-knot *Santa Maria* was completed in 1953 and was used initially on the Brazilian run, to Recife, Rio de Janeiro, and Santos. Her Caribbean sailings began a year later and then the extended service to Florida, then quite a novelty in trans-Atlantic travel, was introduced in October 1956. Also, utilizing only her first and cabin class quarters, she ran

SUNSHINE ALL THE WAY EUROPE FROM MIAMI

T/V SANTA MARIA

VIA THE SUNSHINE ROUTE TO SPAIN AND PORTUGAL

C. C. N.— the Portuguese Line

Mid-Atlantic passages onboard Portugal's *Santa Maria*. (*Author's Collection*)

periodic cruises out of Lisbon to Madeira and into the Mediterranean, and from La Guaira to the Caribbean isles.

The hijacking took place after *Santa Maria* had departed from La Guaira. An armed band of Portuguese political insurgents, traveling as passengers, took command of the ship. Radio connections were stopped and, for several days, her whereabouts were unknown. A huge air-sea search was mounted before the ship was finally surrendered without any loss of life or damages. She was returned to her owners at Recife in Brazil and where the terrorists were arrested.

Luis Miguel Correia, Portugal's foremost maritime historian, recalled the event:

Captain Henrique Galvao and his team of twenty-four Portuguese and Spanish rebels, operating from a base in Venezuela, decided to attack a passenger ship from one of the Iberian nations to protest against the dictatorships of Franco in Spain and Salazar in Portugal. The *Santa Maria* was selected because she was by far the largest and best ship, although two Spanish passenger liners, the *Covadonga* and *Guadalupe*, were also considered. The rebels' intention was to sail the ship to the island of Fernando Po, in Spanish Guinea in West Africa. Once there, they hoped to seize the Island and eventually launch an attack on Portuguese Angola. Realistically, I think that Captain Galvao only hoped to get the international press to pay attention to those Iberian dictatorships.

The *Santa Maria* later resumed her Caribbean–Florida crossings, but inevitably grew older and less profitable, especially in the face of increased airline competition. Luis Miguel Correia recalled the end of the then twenty-year-old ship:

She arrived at Lisbon for the last time in April 1973, with engine troubles. Major repairs would have been impractical. And so, this was just enough to finish her off. Temporarily repaired, she departed a month later on a cargo-only voyage to Luanda and Lourenco Marques. She carried general cargo as well as dozens of automobiles, many of which were stowed on her outer decks. Once at Lourenco Marques, she had one last duty to perform. She towed two small Companhia Colonial freighters to a scrap yard in Mauritius. Afterward, she sailed empty and with a small crew to Taiwan, where she herself was scrapped. It was the end for Portugal's *Santa Maria*.

Above: Farewell to Europe and bound for South America: The aft decks of Costa Line's *Federico "C"*. (*Author's Collection*)

Below: Argentina created passenger ships of its own for services to/from Europe including the 11,000-ton *Yapeyu*, shown being constructed in Holland in 1951. (*Cronican-Arroyo Collection*)

Spain's Naviera Aznar—also known as the Aznar Line—traded to the Canary Islands but also to the East Coast of South America. (*Author's Collection*)

4

TO DISTANT, DARKEST AFRICA

Union-Castle

Unquestionably, the best known and best remembered liner company in service to Africa was Britain's Union-Castle Line. In 1960, they were running as many as thirteen passenger liners—the 37,600-grt *Windsor Castle* was the largest, fastest, and best of the fleet, followed by the *Pendennis Castle, Pretoria Castle, Edinburgh Castle, Capetown Castle, Stirling Castle, Athlone Castle, Carnarvon Castle, Rhodesia Castle, Kenya Castle, Braemar Castle, Durban Castle*, and *Warwick Castle*. The *Bloemfontein Castle* had just been sold off and the new *Transvaal Castle* was due in late 1961.

First class aboard the Union-Castle Line was well known, being frequented by government officials, business tycoons and even occasional royalty. Britain's Princess Alice, the last granddaughter of Queen Victoria, was a regular in the 1950s and '60s. 'It was all classic ocean travel,' recalled Alan Parkhurst. 'Morning deck games, a long lunch followed by a long nap, tea at four and then little more than dancing, horse racing or a film after dinner. It was all very gentile, almost unchanged from times past.'

Migrants were also an important part of Union-Castle's liner trade to Africa. John Jones also served aboard Union-Castle's *Bloemfontein Castle*, an all-tourist-class ship designed purposely for immigrants and low-fare travelers. 'We carried lots of British migrants going out to Rhodesia, but also stopped in Rotterdam and collected Dutch and German migrants as well. Often, they were very poor people. When we'd reach Africa, on their last day onboard, they'd steal food from the dining room. They had no money for food for even their first days ashore.'

Elder Dempster Lines

In the 1960s, in those waning days of the once vast British Empire, the last colonial or commonwealth passenger ship links still hung-on. While P&O looked after India and Australia, and the British India Line traded to East Africa, Liverpool-based Elder Dempster Lines took care of the passenger and cargo service to West Africa—to ports like Lagos, Takoradi, and Tema in places like Ghana and Nigeria. George Munn, now long-retired and a fellow passenger aboard a cruise to the Mediterranean, was the assistant chief engineer aboard the small passenger ship, *Accra*. Small by any standard at only 12,000 tons and carrying only some 275 one-class passengers (plus lots of cargo as well), she was teamed with her twin sister, the *Apapa*, and larger, fancier company flagship, the *Aureol*. By the early '60s, when George joined Elder Dempster, business was still quite good, even quite profitable—and there were still passengers travelling by sea:

The *Accra* was very quaint in lots of ways. Onboard, she looked like yesteryear with her 1940s décor and had a very quiet, almost sedate atmosphere. As an assistant chief engineer, I ate in the passenger dining room. We had all sorts of passengers going and coming—civil servants, doctors, engineers, students. The chief purser always checked

Above: The 18,500-ton *Bloemfonetin Castle* was all one-class, created in 1950 especially for the East African migrant trade. (*Richard Faber Collection*)

Left: Union-Castle Line offered a historic, very well-known and highly popular service to South and East African ports from the UK. Their final big liner was the 32,000-grt *Transvaal Castle* of 1961. (*Andrew Kilk Collection*)

Below: The handsome-looking *Accra* at the Princes Landing Station, Liverpool, preparing for her maiden voyage to West African ports in 1947, with Cunard's *Ascania* to the left. (*Richard Faber Collection*)

Above: The *Aureol* was the popular flagship of Elder Dempster's fleet. (*Author's Collection*)

Right: The West African sailings of Elder Dempster were popular winter escapes. (*Author's Collection*)

THERE **IS** SOMETHING *NEW* UNDER THE SUN

For a delightfu and nterest ng change try the West African sunsh ne this winter

Modern passenger ners eave Liverpool fortnightly on a month's round trip of 8,000 captivating m es to Ghana Nigeria and Sierra Leone, with cal s at Las Palmas and, accord ng to sh p, L beria and the Gambia. The voyage is a hol day n itself

You can have a short stay at a first class hotel in either Accra or Lagos plus al the joys of an ocean voyage—from £235 depend ng on accommodation

★ VACANCIES NOVEMBER TO APRIL INCLUSIVE.

★ ILLUSTRATED FOLDER AND FURTHER DETAILS FROM -

ELDER DEMPSTER LINES

INDIA BUILDINGS, LIVERPOOL 2.
CENtral 8421

SERVICE BY SEA

for unattached ladies and we rotated having them at our tables. But sometimes it backfired—the unattached ladies were, on second glance, seventy or eighty years old. We carried Africans too. But sometimes white passengers refused to sit at the same table with black passengers.

In deep winter, in January and February, we had two special groups of passengers that traveled with us. We had the 'bookies,' from the race courses and the betting parlors, which were then closed for the winter. They would board either the *Accra, Apapa,* or *Aureol* in Liverpool, make the five-day sea journey to Las Palmas, where we always stopped for fuel and water, and then leave the ship and stay ashore in hotels for eight nights. Then they'd catch the northbound ship, for a five-day trip back to the UK. But these 'bookies' could be a problem. We had horse-racing in the lounge and each wooden horse had a name and a jockey. The bookies were given odds so as to place their bets. But they soon figured out that the odds were stacked in favor of the chief purser. The bookies would become most upset and complain bitterly. They were known onboard as the 'wise guys'. The second group were the Blackpool landladies. They ran small hotels and boarding houses, but which were closed in winter as well. It was a time before cheap package holidays to Spain by air and so they used the Elder Dempster ships to and from Las Palmas. These landladies could be quite spirited, however, and were known on Elder Dempster as the 'good time girls'. There were other tourists as well, but West Africa was generally known as the last resort for liner passengers who'd been everywhere.

We also carried deck passengers between the West African ports, mostly women, who were really 'travelling salesmen,' and with their babies and children in tow. They travelled in the fore deck, under a canvas tent covering the two forward cargo holds. They did their own cooking there, had very basic toilet facilities in the deckhouse and were kept away from 'regular' passenger areas by shipboard security. They travelled from port to port, between Lagos, Takoradi and Freetown, selling their goods. Elder Dempster made extra monies by carrying these African deck passengers.

We carried cargo as well and we'd load and offload for ten days at the Liverpool docks. It was all a 'slow discharge'. The Elder Dempster crews went home on leave and the ships were left in the hands of a small standby crew. Outbound to West Africa, we carried lots of mail, manufactured goods and government cargos, which were usually pilfered both in Africa as well as the UK. Homeward to Liverpool, we carried fruits and oils, and refrigerated cargos such as bananas and fruits. We'd also load wickerwork in the Canaries as well as new potatoes and tomatoes. We'd also buy cheap Champagne in Las Palmas and then serve it to the passengers.

George Nunn left Elder Dempster in the early 1960s to join another well-known shipping firm of the time, the Blue Funnel Line. He concluded, 'Blue Funnel was said to be superior in all ways and looked down on Elder Dempster as the "monkey run".'

Lloyd Triestino

Italy's Lloyd Triestino also sailed to Africa, but to the East and South coasts. It is one of the world's oldest shipping firms, dating from 1837, and was housed until the 1980s in a 'grand palazzo' in Trieste. It was said to be more of a maritime museum than shipping office. The collection was quite extraordinary: enormous oil paintings, highly detailed models, and gleaming brass nautical fixtures and fittings.

Until the 1970s, Lloyd Triestino ran passenger ship services on three routes: Italy–Australia, Italy–Far East and Italy–South and East Africa. Beginning in 1957, Captain Lorenzo Calvillo sailed aboard the handsome liners of Lloyd Triestino. 'I served on almost all the company's passenger ships, including the *Africa,* which sailed from Trieste and Venice, through the Suez Canal and to ports down to East and then South African ports.' Carrying 148 first class and 298 tourist class passengers, the exact routing for the 11,500-grt *Africa* and her twin sister *Europa* was from Trieste, Venice, and Brindisi to Port Said, Suez, Aden, Mogadishu, Mombasa, Dar-es-Salaam, Beira, Durban, Cape Town, Port Elizabeth, East London, and then returning via the same East African ports.

Captain Calvillo recalled the *Africa*:

The *Africa* was a beautiful ship, and which handled very well in even the worst weather. We treated her and her sister with tender, loving care—like new brides. There were lots of diplomats and civil servants aboard in those years. The airplane was not yet a threat. Once, we had Mussolini's daughter Edda onboard. She had a farm in Kenya. She bought lots of things from vendors at Port Said, just before we entered the Suez Canal. I brought them to her stateroom and she rewarded me with a single yellow rose, which I actually kept, pressed in plastic, until very recently [1995]. We also called at Mogadishu in Somalia, but then an Italian territory. We anchored offshore and used to take on and discharge our passengers, three or four at a time, in big, round, canvas baskets called 'mamicias'. Cargo cranes on deck did the lifting and lowering.

Above left: Very modern and handsome ships, the sisters *Europa* (shown) and *Africa* were among the best-fitted liners in African passenger service in the 1950s and '60s. (*Robert Pabst Collection*)

Above right: Portugal has sizeable interest in African passenger services and these included the 1948-built sisters *Patria* and *Imperio* of Lisbon-based Companhia Colonial. (*Companhia Colonial*)

Below right: A first class cabin aboard another Portuguese liner, the 1955-built *Uige*. (*Companhia Colonial*)

5

BEYOND SUEZ:
INDIA AND OTHER EASTERN ROUTES

Blue Funnel Line

Far Eastern waters! John Morgan worked back in the 1960s for Britain's Blue Funnel Line. He was assigned to *Ixion*, a sturdy passenger-cargo liner that carried nearly three dozen all-first class passengers on the long-haul run from Liverpool out to the Far East, to Singapore, Hong Kong, Kobe, and Yokohama. He also served aboard the same company's *Pyrrhus*, which was on the Australian run out of Liverpool—steaming off to Fremantle, Melbourne, and Sydney.

I was a bathroom steward and my daily duties included scheduling the passengers bathing, running a tub and then cleaning it afterward. There were very few private bathrooms attached to cabins in those days and instead passengers used public facilities located along the corridor. Little rooms with polished wood doors contained bathtubs. My duties included supplying a fresh towel. Even with as few as thirty passengers, it wasn't very difficult. Some passengers bathed only every other day or even every third day back then.

Anchor Line

The smell of curry! 'They were said to be the best kept, most immaculate passenger ships using the port of Liverpool in the 1950s and '60s,' said Mike McDougle, who served aboard Britain's long-gone Anchor Line and aboard the company's three 11,000-ton passenger ships, the *Caledonia, Cilicia,* and *Circassia*, which carried up to 300 one-class passengers each.

We were on the Indian run—sailing by way of Gibraltar, Port Said and the Suez Canal to Karachi and, the final stop, to Bombay. We carried very few tourists actually, but mostly government people, lots of the old colonials, businessmen, tea merchants and Indians including the occasional maharaja. Those Indian princes traveled with entire entourages that occupied as many as a dozen cabins onboard. One royal, I think it was the Maharaja of Rawalpindi, had a stateroom just for his pet falcon.

These Anchor liners were famed for their cuisine. They had all-Indian galley crews that prepared the most wonderful curries. Just having, say, lunch aboard at Liverpool was a treat. Anchor Line food was equal to the finest Indian restaurant. Anchor was also noted for its exceptional maintenance and shipboard care. Everything, even the engine room, was in pristine condition. Even though these ships were over twenty years of age, it was as if they'd just left the shipyard.

British India Line

It was, until the 1970s, well-known in ports in Africa, India, the Middle and Far East as 'BI'—the British India Steam Navigation

Company Limited. They were a key part of the old British Empire, the imperial chain, as steady reliable links for the flow of both passengers and cargo. The passengers were themselves often representatives of the Crown: the governors and high commissioners, the police and military, civil servants, their families, the merchants and the traders, traveling colonials and the occasional tourist.

BI had a very large fleet of passenger ships in the 1950s—fourteen in all. There were the sisters *Amra* and *Aronda*, which served on two of the company's more important services: from Bombay and Karachi to East Africa, to Mombasa and Dar-es-Salaam, and from Karachi to Chittagong via Colombo. The four smaller D Class ships—*Dumra, Dara, Dwarka,* and *Daressa*—handled the local Persian Gulf trade out of Bombay and Karachi. The trio named *Sangola, Santhia,* and *Sirdhana* worked the Far Eastern trade—from Calcutta to Rangoon, Penang, Singapore, Hong Kong, Kobe, and Yokohama. The aged *Rajula*, built in 1926 and sailing for almost fifty years, singlehandedly looked after the Bay of Bengal run—between Madras, Nagapattinam, Penang, and Singapore. Then there was the very popular pair of 10,300-grt sisters, the *Kampala* and *Karanja*, which traded between India and East Africa—from Bombay and Karachi to the Seychelles, Mombasa, Zanzibar, Dar-es-Salaam, Beira, Lourenco Marques, and Durban. Finally, there were the 14,400-grt sisters *Kenya* and *Uganda*, which ran the mainline service from London via Gibraltar, Marseilles, Malta, Port Said and the Suez Canal to Aden, Mombasa, Tanga, Zanzibar, Dar-es-Salaam, and Beira.

Brian Gregory, a former junior engineer aboard British India, recalled the aged *Rajula* and her Eastern sailings between Madras and Singapore:

She was a beautiful old ship, in fact a very easy ship to run. We carried thirty in first class [1965] or what might be better described as 'those passengers with cabins'. There were only about a dozen Europeans each year; the rest were rich Indians. In this area of the ship, there was what we called forced-air ventilation. From everywhere, cool air blew into the cabin areas. The ship's biggest revenues came, however, from the 1,600 deck passengers [there were also berths in second class, 133 in all]. These deck passengers were Indians going backwards and forwards, mostly to work in the Malaysian rubber plantations and tin mines. The Indians were the laborers. During an eight-day passage between Madras and Singapore, they lived in a protected space known

as 'tween decks'. Often, however, and in the hottest weather, they slept on the open decks. Understandably, there was a need for fresh air. Originally, these deck passengers did their own cooking, but this was later replaced by a ship's canteen that served only Indian food.

The *Rajula* was almost always filled to capacity. She was of course a rather small passenger ship, weighing in at 8,500 tons. Every voyage, she had 1,500 or more passengers onboard. She had a guaranteed income. I recall that she had all-British officers to the very end of her British India days [she was finally scrapped at Bombay in 1975], except for the pursers, who were Goans. Another little oddity that I remember from the *Rajula* was that her chief steward was called 'the butler'.

Lloyd Triestino

Italy's Lloyd Triestino ran Middle and Far Eastern passenger services in the 1950s and '60s as well. Captain Lorenzo Calvillo served aboard the *Asia*, which together with sistership *Victoria*, sailed in East of Suez service. He recalled:

We sailed primarily between Italy, India and Hong Kong. [Genoa, Naples, Port Said, Suez, Aden, Karachi, Bombay, Colombo, Singapore and Hong Kong.] We had mostly British passengers back in the 1950s as well as German and Swiss business people. There were also Eastern merchants, the clergy and missionaries, and even the odd sultan, who usually took three or four cabins and brought along his own servants and bodyguards. On the three-week trips out to Hong Kong, we also had lots of cargo—Italian dresses, leather shoes and auto parts. Homeward to Italy, we carried mostly inexpensive goods made in Japan but trans-shipped to Hong Kong. These included a large amount of toys, plastic umbrellas—those little novelties.

Above: Great favorites on the Indian run from the UK were the three Anchor liners *Cilicia* (shown), *Circassia*, and *Caledonia*. (*Alex Duncan*)

Right: The Anchor liners were popular not only with British but Indian and Pakistani passengers as well. (*Author's Collection*)

Below: Tropic refuge: The first class bar aboard the *Cilicia*. (*Author's Collection*)

ANCHOR LINE

INDIA PAKISTAN

CALLING AT
GIBRALTAR
PORT SAID—ADEN

Right: Divided ship: The 8,500-ton *Sirdhana* of British India could carry three classes of passengers—first, second, and third/deck class. (*British India Line*)

Below left: Life aboard British India in the 1960s. (*British India Line*)

Below right: British India passenger ships were great links, reminders even, between life in England and voyaging among African and Eastern ports. (*British India Line*)

elaxation...

● TOURIST SMOKING ROOM

Luxury...

● TOURIST DINING SALOON

● FIRST CLASS DE LUXE CABIN WITH BATH

B·I

Superb Service...

- Fully-equipped Hospital
- Shopping facilities
- Children's Hostess
- Entertainment
- Two Swimming pools
- Acres of Sun and Promenade Decks
- Two spacious Drawing Rooms
- Deck Sports
- Two elegant Dining Rooms
- Dance Orchestra
- Two Smoking Rooms

- Superb Cuisine
- Movies
- Cocktail Lounge
- Outside cabins
- Hairdressing Saloon

ard Room
wo Libraries
Writing Room and Chapel
hildren's Dining Room
Verandah Ballroom
wo Nurseries
aundry Service plus Ironing and Drying Rooms

Whether
**First or
Tourist Class**

You can
be assured of

**First Class
Service**

B·I

● FIRST CLASS DINING SALOON

● FIRST CLASS DRAWING ROOM

Sailing out to the Far East from Italian ports were the smart-looking sister ships *Asia* and *Victoria*. (*Robert Pabst Collection*)

On the run to the former Dutch East Indies were ships such as the Nederland Line's *Johan van Oldenbarnevelt*. (*Richard Faber Collection*)

Right: Another Dutch firm, the Royal Interocean Lines, ran a long-haul service between South America, South Africa, and the Far East. (*Author's Collection*)

Below: Dutch liners used in Eastern services, especially Indonesia, all but cram docks at Rotterdam. In this view from May 1954, the *Willem Ruys*, flagship of the Royal Rotterdam Lloyd, takes center stage with two other passenger ships (the *Indrapoera* and *Waterman)* among several freighters. (*Richard Faber Collection*)

6

'NEW AUSTRALIA' BECKONS

P&O Liners of the 1950s

'Back in the 1950s and '60s, P&O filled their older liners with lots of low-fare passengers,' recalled Geoff Gardner, a regular passenger aboard a number P&O liners in the 1950s.

There were the ten-pound Brits, who were emigrating to places like Fremantle, Melbourne and Sydney. These were usually six-week voyages down from London or Southampton. But P&O also carried other migrants, Italians and Greeks [boarding at Naples and Piraeus], and cabins were allocated just for them. Some Brits were actually upset because they couldn't get a berth on a P&O ship and so had to come out to Australia on Italian or Greek ships, which they felt were inferior. P&O also had a large Australian tourist business back in those days. It was a rite of passage for young Australians to start work, then receive a six-month leave and visit Britain and Europe. The great cultural link between Australia and England was still very, very strong. For many, it was ancestral roots. Myself, I was an Australian citizen and a British subject. I well remember some of the older P&O liners used in all-one class migrant service. I'd see them berthed at Sydney. The *Orontes* was the eldest, being commissioned back in 1929. She was classic looking—with two, pencil-like funnels and a black hull. To me, she seemed very grand on the inside, even in her later, reduced-fare days. The dining room still had frescoes and wall decorations. It was actually quite palatial for the Aussie run. Those old liners were not air-conditioned and were virtual infernos, especially when in the Red Sea and crossing the Indian Ocean. A crew man told me that when the ships were anchored at Aden, young crew members would dive off the bow and have a cooling swim. The *Stratheden*, dating from 1937, was a great favorite of mine. She had an especially tall, single funnel and this gave her added good looks. The *Orion* from 1935 was decoratively revolutionary in her time. She was the first 'real' Art Deco liner on the Australian run. That design had not been heard of in Australia back in the '30s. She was actually considered ultra-modern for her time. Even to the end of her days, it seemed that everything about her fitted into place and was all very functional. In the 1960s, many preferred older liners like the *Orion* and *Stratheden* to the then new age of the *Canberra* and *Oriana*.

P&O built a new generation of bigger, larger, better equipped liners just after the Second World War. These ships were purposely intended for the Aussie run—regular 'line voyages' from London or Southampton to Gibraltar, Marseilles, the Suez Canal, Aden, Colombo, Fremantle, Melbourne, and Sydney. The *Himalaya* of 1948 was a direct descendant of the Strath class of the 1930s and especially the *Stratheden* of 1937. Clearly, some of the same blueprints were used. The *Chusan* was very similar to the *Himalaya*, but slightly smaller and therefore more intimate in feel. Although designed especially for the UK–Far East run, she made many, many trips to Australia. To Aussies, she had an added personality—she was P&O's 'different ship'. The *Arcadia* and *Iberia* were the big sensations of the mid-1950s. They were a step up and even looked right, like proper ships. In Australia, the *Arcadia* was always more popular. She had the better onboard feel, it was said. It was also said that she always had the better crew as well. The *Iberia* was somehow never quite right, never worked quite as well and also had mechanical problems.

'The *Arcadia* was my favorite P&O liner of all,' said Howard Franklin, another longtime passenger aboard the great P&O Lines, one of the most illustrious shipping lines and still sailing today but as Carnival Corporation-owned P&O Cruises. P&O liners touched on over 100 ports in all.

Beginning just after the Second World War, P&O built a series of what were then large, quite fast liners for the mainline operation: from London to Sydney via the Suez route. The itineraries usually included Gibraltar, Marseilles, Port Said, Aden, Colombo, Fremantle, and then Melbourne. Business boomed, for passengers as well as some high grade freight and the all-important mails, and so newer, bigger ships were the order of the day. Trading was also heavily sparked by a brisk business with mostly post-war British immigrants, including full families, who were then seeking new lives in opportunity-rich Australia. 'Life Down Under' seemed to be like a paradise. In some years, in the 1950s and into the '60s, as many as 100,000 Brits headed for Australian shores and new lives. That vast continent beckoned as so-called 'New Australia'.

Preparing for the demands in that pre-jet age, London-based P&O built four new liners in succession: the *Himalaya* (1949), the *Chusan* (1950), and then the *Arcadia* and *Iberia* (1954). 'They were wonderful ships, but for me, the *Arcadia* had something special about her,' remembered Howard Franklin:

She had the most wonderful library with club chairs. You can just curl-up and read a good book. P&O ships differed from their close rivals, the big liners of the Orient Line, which was also British. P&O was more equalitarian. There was less aristocracy in first class, for example. Orient Line ships felt like big country houses gone to sea while P&O liners were more hotels at sea. Orient Line also had better food and impeccable service in first class, which was superior to P&O.

Shaw Savill Line

Their motto was 'Ship and travel Shaw Savill'. They were one of Britain's best known, most popular, and more successful liner companies. By the late 1950s, they were running the innovative *Southern Cross*, the splendid but older *Dominion Monarch* and four combo ships—the *Athenic, Gothic, Corinthic,* and *Ceramic.*

Keith Hickey recalls:

She was one of the finest and most popular ships ever to sail in Australian service. The *Dominion Monarch*, built just before the War, in 1939, belonged to the Shaw Savill Line. She was actually a large, luxurious passenger-cargo vessel. She carried just 500 or so passengers, all in first class, on the very long run between England, South Africa, Australia and then over to New Zealand. The full roundtrip took three-and-a-half months back in the 1950s. I remember seeing her during her overnight stays in Sydney harbor. She was a very handsome ship. She had perfect proportions. She had a white superstructure set upon a black hull. She was actually quite different, even unusual. I was never sure if she was a liner or a big passenger-cargo ship. From several visits, I recall she was very beautiful on the inside. She was always spotless, shining from end to end. She was very British, very clubby, very high standard. I remember there were lots of big, old, stuffed chairs and fireplaces. It was the kind of ship where one had coffee in the lounge after dinner.

After a gap when he sailed aboard freighters, John Jones was soon back to passenger ships by the mid-1950s. He continued to be that 'gypsy' and sailed aboard Shaw Savill Line, Union-Castle, New Zealand Shipping Company, and the exotic Booth Line. At Shaw Savill, he sailed in two of the company's oldest, if smaller, liners:

The *Mataroa* and *Tamaroa*, used on the long-haul New Zealand run, were two of the oldest and slowest passenger ships in the British fleet by then [they were retired in the late 1950s]. It took six weeks to go from London to Auckland via Curacao and the Panama Canal. Occasionally, we'd stop at Pitcairn Island to land supplies and mail. The locals, who were expert rowers, would come out to the anchored ship in open boats. They were very spiritual people. Once, these open boats were caught in a fierce, tropical storm. They all continued to row as they sang hymns. After arriving in New Zealand, we'd stay in local ports for six weeks, mostly loading lamb to be brought back to England. I made extra money by working as a temporary docker. But once I missed the ship and was taken to jail as a deserter. The jail for two nights was

Above: One of P&O's finest and most popular post-war liners, the 28,000-ton *Himalaya*, as seen in the London Docks. (*P&O*)

Left: The migrant trade: Passengers at Marseilles aboard P&O's *Maloja* in a view dating from 1948.

Post-war British liner decor: The First Class Observation Lounge aboard the *Himalaya*, commissioned in 1949. (*P&O*)

Cut the winter

TAKE A P&O-ORIENT VOYAGE TO THE SUNNY SIDE OF THE WORLD

Spend this winter in the sun. A P&O–Orient voyage will give you two, three months or more of sun, sea air, relaxation and perfect comfort.

P&O ORIENT LINES

Above left: One of P&O's favorite liners, the mighty *Arcadia*, arriving off Suva on Fiji. (*P&O*)

Above right: Another escape route from the dreary British winters: P&O voyages down to Australia and New Zealand. (*Author's Collection*)

Ships such as the 29,000-ton, 1,500-passenger *Arcadia* had lots of open deck areas because of their normally tropical sailings. In this view, however, the 721-foot-long ship is visiting New York as part of a cruise in September 1959. (*Moran Towing & Transportation Co.*)

HONGKONG by P&O

Exotic destinations: An evocative P&O baggage label from the 1950s. (*Author's Collection*)

Above: The 41,000-ton *Oriana*, commissioned in December 1960, had the record: She could sail from Southampton to Sydney in twenty-one days, thereby cutting seven days off the previous record. (*Luis Miguel Correia*)

Right: Dining pleasure: A menu from 1961 aboard the *Arcadia*. (*Author's Collection*)

TOURIST

LUNCHEON

SCOTCH BROTH

FRIED HAKE, RÉMOULADE SAUCE

STEAK AND KIDNEY PUDDING

MACARONI MILANAISE

VEGETABLES

POTATOES: BOILED   CREAMED
BRUSSELS SPROUTS

COLD SIDEBOARD

PRESERVED BRISKET   GAME PIE

SALAD
MIXED SALAD

SWEETS
FRESH STRAWBERRIES WITH CREAM   COFFEE ICE

CHEESES
TAFFEL   DANISH BLUE

BISCUITS   COFFEE

TEA AND COFFEE IS SERVED IN ALL PUBLIC ROOMS

A VEGETARIAN MENU IS AVAILABLE ON REQUEST TO THE
HEAD WAITER OR DEPUTY PURSER

S.S. "ARCADIA"   FRIDAY, 16TH JUNE, 1961

P & O Cruises   **s.s. ORIANA**

Programme of

THE ORIANA CUP
HORSE RACE MEETING

After twenty six years of continuing
events, the Oriana Jockey Club holds
its final meeting this evening,
Friday March 21 1986

by kind permission of

CAPTAIN PHILIP JACKSON

———————

$1 Tote will operate on all Races

$2 Tote Double on Races 3 and 5
and THE ORIANA CUP

Your Race Commentator:
MATTHEW McLAUCHLAN

Above: Out to the East: P&O's combo liners *Cathay* and *Chitral* (shown) carried about 250 all-first class passengers on the run between London and Far Eastern ports. (*Alex Duncan*)

Left: Life aboard: Horse racing aboard the *Oriana*. (*Lindsay Johnstone Collection*)

On her post-Coronation Tour of 1953–54, Queen Elizabeth II and her entourage used Shaw Savill's eighty-five-passenger *Gothic* as a substitute royal yacht. She is seen here with some of the staff aboard the 15,000-ton ship. (*Shaw Savill Line*)

SHAW SAVILL LINE

FIRST CLASS
ACCOMMODATION PLAN

QUADRUPLE SCREW MOTOR VESSEL

"DOMINION MONARCH"
26,500 TONS

SCRAPPED

It's FUN to TRAVEL

SHAW SAVILL

This booklet comes to you with the compliments of

William H. Miller
1235 Park Avenue
Hoboken, N.J

Agents for the SHAW SAVILL LINE

Above left: The all-first class *Dominion Monarch* was a very popular ship on the extended run from the UK to Australia and New Zealand via South Africa. (*Lindsay Johnstone Collection*)

Above right: The *Southern Cross* of 1955 represented a new style for a modern liner: All one-class, engines aft and no cargo whatsoever. (*Andrew Kilk Collection*)

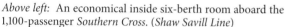

Above left: An economical inside six-berth room aboard the 1,100-passenger *Southern Cross*. (*Shaw Savill Line*)

Above right: The aft section of the 20,000-ton *Southern Cross*, the beginning of a new design for larger liners. (*Shaw Savill Line*)

Right: Bargain travel: An advert for inexpensive sea travel on Shaw Savill liner to/from Australia and New Zealand. (*Author's Collection*)

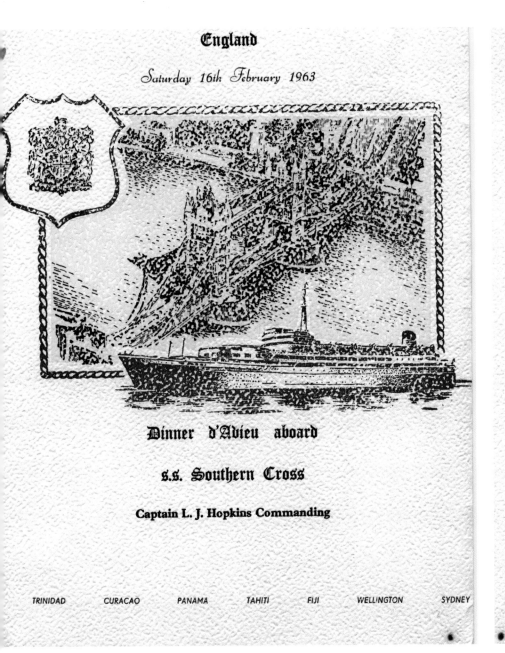

England

Saturday 16th February 1963

Dinner d'Adieu aboard

s.s. Southern Cross

Captain L. J. Hopkins Commanding

TRINIDAD   CURACAO   PANAMA   TAHITI   FIJI   WELLINGTON   SYDNEY

MELBOURNE   FREMANTLE   DURBAN   CAPETOWN   LAS PALMAS   SOUT

Menu

Chilled Grapefruit Maraschino
Consomme Sherry   Potage Milanai
Fillet of Lemon Sole, Maitre d'Hotel
Butter Beans & Tomatoes
Filet Mignon, Calcutta
Leg & Shoulder of Mutton, Redcurrant Jel
Roast Turkey & Seasoned Forcemeat
Brussels Sprouts
Roast, Boiled & Garfield Potatoes

COLD BUFFET

Roast Pork   Liver Sausag

Salads: Mexican

Dressings: French Mayonnaise Cranberry

SWEET

Plum Pudding, Rum Sauce
Pineapple Sundae
Vanilla Ice Cream

Savoury: Canape Radjah

Dessert

Coffee will be served in Public Rooms

MELBOURNE   FREMANTLE   DURBAN   CAPETOWN   LAS PALMAS   SOUT

Above left and right: Dinner menu aboard the *Southern Cross*, dated February 1963.

Larger than the *Southern Cross*, the 1,400-passenger *Northern Star* was added to the around-the-world service in 1961. (*Albert Wilhelmi Collection*)

awful—a straw mattress for a bed and meager rations for food. After I was freed, I was flown—and under police guard—to the South Island to rejoin the *Mataroa*. I was taken aboard, brought before the captain and fined a week's pay plus the cost for the jail, police, and plane ride. I returned to London with no money—not a penny!

Just after the Second World War, Shaw Savill had decided to continue with passenger ships that had a pre-war, club-like atmosphere, but in far smaller vessels and with far less accommodation. Four combination passenger-cargo liners, to be called *Corinthic, Athenic, Gothic,* and *Ceramic,* with space for eighty-five first passengers only, were ordered. The 15,000-grt *Corinthic,* the first of the quartet, was launched in May 1946 and was commissioned eleven months later.

These ships plied an extended service—from London to Curacao and the Panama Canal, and then onwards to ports only in New Zealand. The late Peter Buttfield, a shipping agent at Sydney, recalled their long-haul services:

They were good little ships, but difficult to load and unload. Often, they would spend as long as eight to ten weeks in New Zealand, offloading general cargo from the UK and then loading meat and freezer cargos. They would arrive at Wellington and then go to Lyttleton, Port Chalmers, occasionally back to Wellington and then to Auckland. Actually, as advertised, posted schedules were very difficult to keep. Also, when in port, we would run tours over these ships for travel agents and perspective passengers. They were marketed to travelers who wanted a 'business class' atmosphere. You might say that they were ideal cabin class or even second class type ships. Comparatively, in the late 1940s, it was £109 to the UK.

Michael Parks recalls his memorable journey onboard Shaw Savill's *Gothic*:

In 1952 and fresh out of naval training school, I was 'boy of the year' and selected for special duty—to go to sea onboard the *Gothic,* a passenger-cargo liner that carried eighty-five first class passengers. She was owned by the Shaw Savill Line and carried general cargo out and refrigerated cargo home on the run between London and ports in New Zealand. We used the Panama route, but then sometimes Suez instead. It was a three-month roundtrip.

At the time, the old royal yacht *Victoria & Albert* was being scrapped and the keel for the new *Britannia* was not yet laid down. King George VI wanted Princess Elizabeth and Prince Philip to do a Commonwealth Tour around the world. So the *Gothic* was refitted at Birkenhead for the royal tour and entourage, the size and intimacy of an eighty-five-passenger ship being just perfect. The *Gothic's* sister ship, the *Ceramic,* had actually been the first choice, but plans changed. I was selected as one of six boys/cadets to join the *Gothic* and the tour.

The *Gothic* had served well and afterward was sent to Liverpool for re-conversion back to a normal commercial ship. A great journey was over!

By the mid-1950s, Shaw Savill had added insight—they saw a great future not only in the UK–Australia passenger trade, but in around-the-world travel and tourism. Keith Hickey, an Australian ocean liner enthusiast, remembered the period:

The *Southern Cross* was the great fore-runner of modern design in big liners. She had her funnel placed far aft and that allowed for open mid ship passenger space. Engines aft was the future. The *Southern Cross* was already big news when she was launched at Belfast in 1954. She was novel for her time—she was all-tourist class. Passengers in a single cabin were the same as those in a six-berth. She was well ahead of her time. She even looked very modern, very contemporary. She had a light violet hull and green upper works at first. She actually looked bright, even tropical. She carried no cargo whatsoever and was a first even for that. She was the very best ship of her time for migrants and low-fare round-trippers.

Appropriately, the 20,000-grt *Southern Cross* was placed on a continuous round-the-world service—making four seventy-six-day voyages that kept to a set itinerary: Southampton to Las Palmas, Cape Town, Durban, Fremantle, Melbourne, Sydney, Auckland, Wellington, Fiji, Tahiti, Panama Canal, Curacao, Trinidad, and then home to Southampton. Passengers could sail for as little as two or three days, book the month or so to Sydney, or make the full voyage.

Others felt positive about the future of the Australian liner trade and beyond. P&O added the *Oriana* and *Canberra* in 1960–61, the Italians were converting more ships and often lavishly, and the Greeks, namely the Chandris Lines, arrived on the scene with refitted liners. Shaw Savill rushed forward with the *Northern Star* of 1962.

The *Northern Star* was a larger, slightly improved version of the *Southern Cross* of 1955. The 24,700-grt ship actually replaced the *Dominion Monarch*, an old veteran that dated from 1939. The *Northern Star* was named at her launch by the Queen Mother and had lots of publicity in her maiden year. But she was always a tender ship, however. She had mechanical difficulties from the start as well. It was even rumored that she was almost lost during her sea trials in the North Sea. From the beginning, she never had the popularity of the *Southern Cross*. She may have been bigger and an improvement in ways, but the *Northern Star* never had the right feel.

Sitmar Line

The Genoa-based Sitmar Line started primarily in the migrant business, from Europe to Australia, but then expanded to a worldwide service. Their general routing by the 1960s was outbound from Southampton to Port Said, Suez, Aden, Fremantle, Melbourne, Sydney, Auckland, Papeete, Balboa, Cristobal, Curacao, Lisbon, and back to Southampton. Their ships were all one-class and basic, but then continually upgraded and improved. There was the 1,460-passenger *Fairsea*, a former 'baby aircraft carrier' dating from 1941; the *Fairsky,* another former wartime carrier; the *Castel Felice*, dating from 1930; and the 1,900-bed *Fairstar*, a former British troopship.

Lloyd Triestino

Captain Lorenzo Calvillo was assigned to the two of the finest and newest liners on the Europe–Australia run, Lloyd Triestino's *Galileo Galilei* and *Guglielmo Marconi*. Twin sisters commissioned in 1963, they carried 1,700 passengers each in the final boom years of Australian liner service.

> We carried many, many Italian as well as Greek immigrants to new lives in Australia. But then, in the 1970s, we began to have fewer and fewer passengers—and then, in a flash, we had almost none. I recall one trip in 1976 with only 300 passengers onboard. And so, by 1979–81, we went cruising only—to Scandinavia, around the Mediterranean and into the Black Sea—for ICI, Italian Cruises International. In the end, we were chartered to a Greek company, Chandris Cruises, and even carried a special Greek supervisor aboard. But in winters, we were laid-up at Genoa. Thirty-five crew and myself looked after the otherwise quiet *Galileo*. We did light maintenance on that empty ship.

Migrant Ships

Beginning in the late 1940s, many ships—including aged liners as well as former freighters, troopships, warships, and even small aircraft carriers—were converted to carry passengers purposely for the increasing Australian migrant scheme. One ship, the *New Australia*, was purposely rebuilt (with 1,600 all-tourist class berths) for the UK–Australia run. She had been a luxury liner, the *Monarch of Bermuda*, built in 1931 and used on the New York–Bermuda cruise trade. She was, however, swept by fire and all but destroyed during her post-war refit (after serving as a troopship) in 1947. She was salvaged in the end, rebuilt as a migrant ship and pressed into service shared between the British and Australian governments, but managed by the experienced Shaw Savill Line. 'She was a very basic ship in almost all ways. There were no high luxuries,' recalled Mary Burns, who emigrated to Melbourne aboard the 20,300-ton liner in 1955. 'My sisters and I shared in an eight-bunk room with other girls. I seem to recall that it took eight weeks to reach Australia, our new home.'

Another noted migrant ship of the post-war years was the former Cunard-White Star liner *Georgic*, a 27,000-tonner that could carry just under 2,000 low-fare, one-class passengers. John Jones was steward onboard in 1953:

> The *Georgic*, which still had damages from being bombed and set afire in the War, was said to be the 'roughest' passenger ship in the entire British fleet. She was really not fit for regular passenger service. Regular Cunard crews did not want to sail aboard her and sometimes there were too few crew. It was said that Cunard would go to prisons in and around Liverpool and gather-up minor criminals to serve onboard. These crew members were known to cause problems such as brawls and problems with the police in ports of call. They once called a sudden strike in Cape Town and would not re-board the ship, and at

Above left: Converted from a small, Second World War aircraft carrier, Sitmar's 11,000-ton *Fairsea* could carry over 1,400 one-class passengers. (*Alex Duncan*)

Above right: The *Castel Felice* had been rebuilt especially for low-fare passenger sailings, having been British India Line's *Kenya* of 1930. (*Gillespie-Faber Collection*)

The 1,450-berth *Fairsky* was another surplus wartime ship rebuilt by Sitmar for low-fare passenger service. (*Luis Miguel Correia*)

The 27,000-ton *Galileo Galilei* and *Guglielmo Marconi* were among the most modern and popular liners on the Italy–Australia run in the 1960s. (*Robert Pabst Collection*)

The cruise liner *Monarch of Bermuda* of 1931 was rebuilt in the late 1940s as the migrant ship *New Australia*. (*World Ship Society*)

another time the ship itself was actually banned from Australian ports. When I served aboard the *Georgic*, we carried 10 pound Poms, those British migrants out to Sydney. Then we sailed up to Malaya, carrying Australian troops. Then it was to Viet-Nam and a charter to the French. We carried troops and evacuees out of troubled French Indo-China. The troops were a rough lot that included wounded, diseased, and some hired Africans. We delivered them on a long, hot voyage to Algiers and then to Marseilles.

By the 1960s, and as the Australian migrant trade continued, liners on that service improved steadily. Ships carrying their low-fare passengers now had added amenities such as full air-conditioning, large lounges and even showrooms, swimming pools and lido decks, and even more cabins and less dormitories, and more cabins with private facilities.

Lauro Line

By 1965, Italy's Lauro Line added two handsomely converted liners, the Dutch *Willem Ruys* and *Oranje*, and transformed the pair into virtual 'new' ships—the restyled and renamed *Achille Lauro* and *Angelina Lauro*.

Captain Adriano Borreani, a native of Naples, was a junior officer aboard the 23,600-grt *Achille Lauro*. Later used as a cruise ship and known worldwide for her terrorist hijacking (in October 1985), she was a two-class ship (152 in first class and well over 1,500 in tourist class) on the run from Europe out to Australia.

We had seventy-day roundtrips—sailing from Rotterdam, Southampton, Genoa, Naples, Messina, Malta and sometimes Beirut via the Suez Canal to Fremantle, Melbourne and Sydney. Afterward, we usually did a small cruise over to New Zealand with mostly young Australians. These trips were very cheap and always full-up.

On the outbound trips from Europe to Australia, we were always packed—as many as 1,735 in all. There were British mostly in first class and then all mixed nationalities in tourist class. Many of these immigrants had their fares paid for them, either by the Australian Government under a resettlement scheme or by local home

organizations. Many of them had little if any luggage—just the clothes they wore. Many of the women were pregnant, even past three months. Once, I remember a Lebanese couple having a baby onboard. She was named Laura for Lauro.

Some passengers waited for as many as ten years before they had an assigned berth. Others were already so old that they died onboard. If one of them died onboard, we usually buried them at sea, especially if the family had no money. We always did this at 2 in the morning, without other passengers seeing it. They were immigrants, bound for a new life in far-off Australia. They were Yugoslavian and Austrian, Polish and Hungarian, Dutch and German, and certainly lots of Italians.

The summer trips in June, July, and August were said to be the most difficult:

The monsoons blowing in the Indian Ocean at that time of year caused much seasickness. There were passengers who stayed for a full week in their cabins. They ate just bread. And they were petrified! There was no way to convince some to come out. And we had so many languages, it was almost impossible to communicate. With the Yugoslavians particularly, we had to use hand language. But when these passengers were well, they ate anything and everything.

These voyages had added amenities and services:

There was always a representative of the Australian Government onboard looking after the needs of these immigrants. They gave talks on Australian life and held classes on basic English words. The various groups usually had one English-speaking person as a relay. Landing in Australia was usually very well planned. Since the immigrants did not have homes, they were first sent to relocation centers but everyone started with a job. These were usually manual, often hard labor tasks, but it was a beginning. There was excellent organization. But Australia was gradually filled. General immigration was closed finally in the 1970s. Only openings for specialist trades were left. All the big Mediterranean passenger firms—Lauro, Lloyd Triestino, Sitmar and Chandris—lost their business.

Even the return passenger trade was eventually slumped. 'Homewards to Europe, we used to have different passengers, often business people,' concluded Captain Borreani. 'About 50 per cent were Europeans returning for visits after several years in Australia. Another 25 per cent were people dissatisfied with Australian life. In all, we might fill 75 per cent of our total capacity.'

The *Achille Lauro* and her fleetmate, the *Angelina Lauro*, were made over as cruise ships in 1973. By then, the era of Australian immigrants by sea was just about over.

The striking-looking *Achille Lauro* at Genoa. She had been the Dutch *Willem Ruys*, dating from 1947 but greatly rebuilt in 1965. (*Steffen Weirauch Collectuion*)

Above: The *Angelina Lauro* had also been Dutch, the former *Oranje* of 1939, and largely rebuilt in the mid-1960s. (*Andy Hernandez Collection*)

Right: The 23,500-ton *Achille Lauro* was quite distinctive looking with her two tall, winged funnels. (*Author's Collection*)

MS. ACHILLE LAURO

Above left: The two Lauro liners were noted for their modern, very Mediterranean style decor. (*Author's Collection*)

Above right: Three Dutch liners—the *Oranje, Willem Ruys,* and *Johan van Oldenbarnevelt*—sailed on an around-the-world passenger service in the late 1950s and early '60s. (*Author's Collection*)

7

ACROSS THE PACIFIC

American President Lines

Soon after the War ended, in 1945–46, the first American passenger ships to appear in otherwise devastated Japanese ports were big troopships like the *General Gordon*. They were government-owned, but operated by the San Francisco-based American President Lines and the ships even wore the Company funnel colors atop their gray-painted hulls. Useful and important ships, they were hardly luxurious, and only minimally comfortable. But then, in 1947–48, the brand new *President Cleveland* and *President Wilson* were introduced. 'These ships were like shining palaces,' according to Hisashi Noma, the noted Japanese maritime expert. He continued:

Everyone in Japan was then living in a very reduced level. Daily life was very hard. There were rations for rice and clothing shortages. Many people were hardly able to exist. So, these gleaming, new President liners were rays of light, rays of hope. With their glowing blue-and-red stacks with their silver eagles and stars, their immaculately painted light gray hulls and their all-white superstructures and upper decks, they were symbols of American power and progress. They were also symbols of hope during their regular visits to Yokohama and Kobe. Gradually, American tourists began arriving aboard them. To us, they seemed to come from another world. American ships were like a big Salvation Army—they brought food, hopes for renewal and were symbols of America's superior technology.

Built by Bethlehem Steel at their Alameda, California yard, the twin 18,962-grt *President Cleveland* and *President Wilson* sailed a six-week roundtrip service: San Francisco and Los Angeles over to Honolulu and then Yokohama, Kobe, Hong Kong, and Manila. First class fares in the early 1950s were $150 for the five days to Honolulu and $550 for the fourteen days to Yokohama. In later years, these sailings would become very popular as roundtrip forty-two-day cruise sailings. But in the late 1940s and throughout the '50s, they were quite possibly the busiest liners on the Pacific, especially since most of American President's pre-war competitors, such as Canadian Pacific and Japan's NYK Line, were either gone or much reduced. The place of these President liners was further celebrated when an American firm created a do-it-yourself plastic model kit of them in 12-inch size. They were also the setting for a 1950s television comedy, *Oh Susanna,* which ran from 1956 until 1960. Starring actresses Gale Storm and Zasu Pitts, these President liners were dubbed *Ocean Queen* in the popular series.

Mr Noma again:

When I would visit these ships at the Yokohama Ocean Terminal in the late 1940s, it seemed that these ships came from Heaven, especially with their beautiful lounges, their luxury, their immaculate condition. Below, in the cabins and dormitories of their third class, they carried many, many Hong Kong-Chinese immigrants to post-war lives in the United States.

Post-war Yankee modern: The 18,500-ton sisters *President Cleveland* (shown) and *President Wilson* were great symbols of late 1940s American design and style. (*Cronican-Arroyo Collection*)

Crossing the Pacific: The swimming pool aboard the 700-passenger *President Cleveland*. (*Richard Faber Collection*)

NYK Line

After the Second World War, Japan was left with only one, comparatively small passenger ship: the 11,000-grt *Hikawa Maru*. She had somehow escaped the destruction that had ruined all other liners in that country's glorious pre-war fleet. Used by the US Navy for a time after VJ Day in August 1945, she was later returned to her original owners, the NYK Line, Nippon Yusen Kaisha of Tokyo. Fifty years later, NYK owned one of the world's largest merchant fleets—over 450 ships in all—as well as three luxurious cruise liners, the *Crystal Symphony*, *Crystal Serenity*, and *Asuka II*. And so, in a way, the little *Hikawa Maru* is their ancestor, their grandmother if you will.

Built at Yokohama in 1930, the 536-foot-long *Hikawa Maru* plied a steady North Pacific passenger and freight run between Yokohama, Kobe, Seattle, and Vancouver. She was a troop transport and then hospital ship during the War years, from 1941 until 1945. 'After 1945, the ship was allowed by American occupation forces to run only in Japanese coastal service between Yokohama and Muroran,' said Hisashi Noma. 'Mostly, she carried food to the devastated Tokyo area. She carried passengers too, but they had to bring their own food aboard. The ship's kitchen cooked it for them, but that was all the ship itself could provide. The five years after the War, until 1950, were very difficult in Japan.'

In 1950, the 16-knot *Hikawa Maru* was allowed to resume service across the Pacific to American ports, but even this was a delayed, gradual process. 'She sailed on the freighter service to New York, traveling via the Panama Canal and then also calling at other US East Coast port,' added Mr Noma. 'Only twelve passenger berths, like a freighter, were used, but only for what were called "exceptional passengers," persons who had business in the USA. Afterward, in 1952, she resumed regular passenger service between Kobe, Yokohama, Seattle and Vancouver.'

Like some other Japanese ship enthusiasts, Mr Noma had hoped that the NYK Line would restart its luxury trans-Pacific service:

By 1960, when the *Hikawa Maru* was retired [and converted to a moored museum ship at Yokohama], the NYK directorate felt that airline travel was the future. Cargo ships were a priority then and a fancy passenger liner was not that important. Besides, NYK needed financial assistance from the Japanese Government for such a project. Actually, for the 1964 Olympic Games at Tokyo, NYK was about to build a 28,000-grt, turbine-driven, 24-knot liner for service to and from San Francisco and Los Angeles. The government had agreed to assist. But soon after, a big typhoon struck Ise Bay and the city of Nagoya. There were huge damages and losses, and so the Japanese Government used the monies there instead. Besides, the airlines were already quite prominent.

P&O-Orient Lines

In 1954, when two of Britain's top ocean liner operators, the P&O Lines and the Orient Line, decided to jointly expand, they looked to the Pacific and, in particular, to the North American West Coast. Long-established on the England–Australia service and linked as well to India, Southeast Asia, and the Far East, their expansion was prompted by having a combined fleet of a dozen or so liners. The Pacific, so their London-headquartered directors thought, was 'the last frontier' of ocean travel. New passengers on new trading routes could be found. And so, when the 27,000-grt *Oronsay* reached Sydney in the spring of 1954, she did not return the traditional way, to London via the Suez Canal, but instead steamed northwards to Los Angeles, San Francisco, and Vancouver. This was the beginning of what would become known as the Orient & Pacific Line, later P&O-Orient Lines and the forerunner to present-day P&O Cruises and Princess Cruises. In the 1950s, the new company marketed their rather unique, but highly diverse global passenger ship network with the slogan: 'Runaway to sea!'

Gradually, the infant company took hold in the minds of travel agents and the traveling public. There were big, two-class, all-white liners with names like *Arcadia*, *Chusan*, *Orsova*, and *Orcades*. First class onboard tended to be British tropical—lots of rattan furniture mixed with the likes of floral print sofas and burl woods; tourist class was more austere, very basic in some places and included touches like exposed piping along the ceilings. However, for as little as $10 a day in a four-berth on the lowest deck in tourist class in the late 1950s, passengers could make voyages from 3 to 103 days: coastwise between Vancouver and California, to and from Australia and New Zealand, the Orient and completely around-the-world (the latter often meant changing ships at some point). Later, this combined P&O-Orient operation offered Panama Canal sailings as well—between the West Coast, the Caribbean, Florida, and England.

Above: Japan's only surviving passenger liner, the 11,000-ton *Hikawa Maru*, of the immediate post-war era. (*Author's Collection*)

Right: Another Pacific liner company was the San Francisco-based Matson Line, which operated four liners: *Lurline, Matsonia, Mariposa,* and *Monterey.* (*Author's Collection*)

Welcome to Hawaii—at Honolulu, at Aloha Pier. (*Richard Faber Collection*)

Night Lights: The exceptional *Canberra* of P&O berthed at Circular Quay, Sydney. (*P&O*)

Joann Hastings was employed at the P&O-Orient offices in San Francisco and then, by the mid-1960s, escorted groups of Americans on long voyages aboard what were essentially 'very British' liners:

On these trips, we really were not cruising. They were 'line voyages' only. I particularly recall a trip on the *Orsova*, a six-month voyage completely around-the-world. I escorted 150 Americans and we went from San Francisco to Australia and then onward to the Suez Canal and Europe. We left the ship at Naples to do some overland touring. But then our six-month journey turned into nine months! We reached London just in time for the big British maritime strike [May–June 1966] and so our three hotel nights in London turned into six weeks. P&O had to pay all the extra hotel bills. Finally, our group had shrunk to fifty by the time the strike was over and the *Orsova* was ready to sail for San Francisco on July 4th. By way of the Caribbean and the Panama Canal, it took another three weeks to reach California, to dock at Pier 35 in San Francisco.

Advertised as the 'biggest bloomin' ships sailing the seven seas,' by the 1960s, the P&O-Orient included the 44,000-grt *Canberra* and 41,000-grt *Oriana*. The pair then ranked as two of the largest liners then afloat.

I especially remember all of these P&O-Orient ships for their smells, particularly the smell of British cooking, that ever-prevailing odor of cooked cabbage. Sailing in many of these liners was all part of a wonderful, youthful experience—my first full exposure to Indian curries and over-cooked vegetables, and to go down the hall to the toilet and to a separate room for a bath.

Gradually, we marketed these line voyages more as cruises and even gave them names like *Jolly Swagman* and *Waltzing Matilda*. Sometimes, the itineraries would run up to 125 days. Our American passengers tended to be older, usually retired and often great characters themselves. They traveled in both classes and I was their link for all ship's matters and for their shore tours.

These services ended by the early 1970s. The ships themselves grew older and less profitable, and their trade gradually extended to P&O's Los Angeles-based arm, Princess Cruises. Thereafter, passengers could sail to Sydney or Hong Kong or London, but on the decks of all-first class 'floating resorts' with names like *Golden Princess, Emerald Princess* and *Royal Princess*. In a way, it is nostalgic—it is still 'Runaway to sea!'

8

EMPTY DECKS:
SOME OF THE LAST PASSENGER SHIPS

Stefan Batory

By the 1960s and '70s, a variety of factors killed off traditional passenger ship services. Mostly, it was fierce competition from the airlines. It was, quite simply, faster to go by air. The first effects began on the Atlantic in the late '50s and then spread elsewhere, to routes east of Suez, within a decade. By 1968, it had become 21 hours from London to Sydney compared to 21 days on the fastest liner or 28–35 days on most others. Furthermore, operating costs of passenger ships increased and were often complicated by difficulties that included frequent strikes from seamen's unions. Many passenger ships also relied on cargo as well and this began going in faster, more efficient container ships. Finally, many of the ships were aging and therefore no longer as efficient and sometimes were in need of expensive, modernizing refits. 'It all seemed to disappear overnight, almost in a flash,' remembered Liverpool-based John Jones, who served on British passenger ships. 'Everything was gone—the passengers, the ships, the docks, and even the companies themselves.'

Several passenger companies continued, however. One was Polish Ocean Lines and their flagship, the 15,000-grt *Stefan Batory*. This ship and the *QE2* were said to be very the last Atlantic liners. Until 1987, the 773-passenger *Stefan Batory* made regular crossings between Montreal, London, Copenhagen, and Gdynia. Passenger ship buffs all but flocked to this flagship of the Polish Ocean Lines for 'lost era' charms: the wood and the brass fittings, the traditionalist trans-

Atlantic. routing, the onboard ambience of quiet days and nights and, as time passed, the realization that her days were obviously numbered. Her owners thought of a replacement, but it was simply too expensive

Safmarine Lines

Another long survivor was the Cape Town-based Safmarine Lines, who planned to revive the UK–South Africa liner run. The last regular service, run jointly by Britain's Union-Castle Line and Safmarine, closed down in 1977. A few years later, in 1984, Safmarine evidently rethought the idea of a passenger ship making traditional line voyages. The company bought the luxurious West German liner *Astor*, built in 1981. According to the late Len Wilton, Safmarine's passenger manager in London,

> The *Astor* was bought by the South Africans because of the prestige of owning a passenger liner, to re-establish the old line voyages and to show the flag. In fact, she proved a disappointment in many ways. Apart from being unprofitable (the former Union-Castle clientele could not be revived), the 20,000-grt ship soon had to be changed to Bahamian registry to avoid political difficulties in some of her ports of call. She was sold within a year, in 1985, going to the East German Government, who renamed her *Arkona*.

Above left: A great favorite in later years: The *Stefan Batory* arriving at Lisbon during a cruise. (*Luis Miguel Correia*)

Above right: Safmarine Lines hoped to re-open the UK–South Africa liner run in the mid-1980s with the 20,000-ton *Astor*. (*Author's Collection*)

Ivaran Lines

Among the other more traditional passenger ship ventures was Norway's Ivaran Lines, which, in 1988, commissioned the eighty-eight-passenger *Americana*. Actually a large containership with luxurious accommodation placed aft, she became the last passenger ship to offer regular voyages between New York and the East Coast of South America. It was also offered as a forty-six-night cruise. Ivaran was actually quite ambitious, hoping to build one or two sister ships to the 19,000-grt *Americana*, but shipbuilding costs were rising rapidly at the time. In fact, the *Americana* herself began to struggle in the complicated matters of ship operation and was sold off by the late 1990s to the Chinese. She last sailed as freighter *Golden Trade* before being scrapped in 2010. Her passenger-carrying days lasted less than ten years.

Queen Elizabeth 2

Cunard's *Queen Elizabeth 2* was, in many ways, the last of a somewhat traditional liner. Said to be a 'folly' when built, she actually developed a large, often very loyal following and endured for thirty-nine years, steaming more miles and carrying more passengers than any big liner in history. Douglass Campbell was aboard for *QE2*'s maiden crossing to New York in May 1969:

> The ship was not completely finished on that trip, but she was still pleasant. She was totally different from what we had come to expect from Cunard. The old *Queen Mary* actually had some features that were better such as the steam room. Today [1998], the *QE2* is in pretty good shape for her age. She still had the best cabins afloat. The staff cuts show, but overall there's a valiant effort. Cunard lives on!

When the much loved *QE2* was retired by Cunard in November 2008, she had an extraordinary record—in thirty-nine years of service, she had steamed more miles, visited more ports, carried more passengers, and earned more money than any big liner in history. She was bought (for $100 million) by Dubai buyers for further use as a floating hotel, museum, and entertainment. Long delays have followed and by 2014 the 963-foot-long liner remains idle.

Queen Mary 2

Many thought that the *QE2* would be the end of the line (she was retired by Cunard and sold to buyers in Dubai in the fall of 2008) and that she would not be replaced. However, the mighty, wealthy, Miami-based Carnival Corporation bought Cunard in 1998 for $600 million and almost immediately added $800 million to build a replacement for the beloved *QE2*. This new ship, commissioned in late 2003 as the *Queen Mary 2*, makes crossings between New York, Southampton and sometimes Hamburg for half the year. She is usually booked to capacity and often with ocean travelers wanting a touch of the 'old days'. In this, the *Queen Mary 2*—while a modern, amenity-filled hotel—succeeds. She is said to be the very last 'true ocean liner'.

In 1996, while aboard a Carnival Cruise Lines' cruise ship, Captain Lorenzo Calvillo looked back on almost fifty years at sea, most of them aboard passenger ships. A very charming, most gracious man, he briefly turned nostalgic and said, 'I'm sentimental for those great days of the old, but now bygone ocean liners. It was a golden era!'

Happily, and while more people are going to sea than ever in history, but aboard cruise ships, there are still many links, many great memories, to that 'golden era'.

Above left: Royal launch: Queen Elizabeth II named Cunard's *Queen Elizabeth 2* at launching ceremonies in September 1967. (*Albert Wilhelmi Collection*)

Above right: Crossing the North Atlantic at nearly 30 knots, the mighty *Queen Elizabeth 2* as seen in 1992. (*Author's Collection*)

Below: The biggest Atlantic liner of all time: The 151,000-ton *Queen Mary 2* during a special visit to Hamburg. (*Cunard Line*)

Above: In tribute to the tenth anniversary of the *Queen Mary 2* in May 2014, to Cunard, to all Atlantic liners, and to ocean liners everywhere, the three Cunard Queens—*Queen Mary 2, Queen Elizabeth,* and *Queen Victoria*—depart in regal procession from Lisbon. (*Cunard Line*)

Right: The author on the occasion of the *Queen Mary 2*'s tenth anniversary, May 2014. (*Cunard Line*)

BIBLIOGRAPHY

Crowdy, Michael & O'Donoghue, Kevin (editors), *Marine News*. Kendal, Cumbria: World Ship Society, 1964–2014

Devol, George & Cassidy, Thomas (editors), *Ocean & Cruise News*. Stamford, Connecticut: World Ocean & Cruise Society, 1980–2014

Dunn, Laurence, *Passenger Liners*. Southampton: Adlard Coles Ltd, 1961

—*Passenger Liners* (revised edition). Southampton; Adlard Coles Ltd, 1965

Haws, Duncan, *Merchant Ships: British India Steam Navigation Company*. Burwash, East Sussex, United Kingdom: TCL Publications, 1987

Kohler, Peter, *Sea Safari: British India S. N. Co. African Ships & Services*. Abergavenny, Gwent, United Kingdom: P. M. Heaton Publishing, 1995

Miller, William H., *British Ocean Liners: A Twilight Era 1960-85*. New York: W. W. Norton & Co, 1986

—*Pictorial Encyclopedia of Ocean Liners, 1864-1994*. Mineola, New York: Dover Publications Inc., 1995

—*Picture History of British Ocean Liners*. Mineola, New York: Dover Publications Inc., 2001

Plowman, Peter, *Australian Cruise Ships*. Sydney, Australia: Rosenberg Publishing Pty Ltd, 2007

Squarey, C. M., *The Patient Talks*. London: Thomas Cook & Company Ltd, 1955